The Edge of Dawn

A study of endtime events leading up to the dawning of the day of the Lord we call the tribulation period.

Charles Hiltibidal
Pastor, Bible Teacher, and Author

I am thrilled to recommend Dr. Hiltibidal's book "The Edge of Dawn" as a much needed source for our hour. I have personally seen the people of Northwest Baptist Church captivated by his preaching on prophecy, as they would sit on the ends of their seats listening to this dear brother rightly divide the Scriptures without compromise while God's Word would expose what is happening in our churches, homes, nation, and around the world. I am excited to hear that he has put his material in print. It is obvious that the LORD has blessed Dr. Hiltibidal's love and desire to study Biblical prophecy in a way that will benefit many for the cause of Christ, truly helping the local church. His insight, experience in archeological works, combined with years of studying prophecy, makes this book a great source for pastors and laymen. With many being concerned with current events, it is a real blessing to recommend "The Edge of Dawn."

Dr. Andrew Edwards III

Northwest Baptist Church

Toledo, Ohio

It is my pleasure to offer this recommendation for Dr. Charles Hiltibidal's new book, "Edge of Dawn." This is an enlightening work, beginning with the prophetic Word of God and bringing the reader to its fulfillment in our modern world of technology. This is an accurate portrayal of current events leading us to anticipate the soon-coming return of our Lord Jesus Christ.

As the author spells out the deplorable conditions in our nation and the world at large, he does not leave us without hope. The central theme is that Jesus and His prophets were right in their prophetic statements, and He is a very present Hope during these desperate times. He is the only Hope for our lost world, and Dr. Hiltibidal makes this clear.

This book will enrich your life and ministry.

Carl E. Baugh,
Creation Evidence Museum

Every Christian should read *The Edge of Dawn*. Dr. Charles Hiltibidal is outstanding in Bible knowledge and delivery of end-time Bible prophecy. He answers the common questions and educates us with his experience of many years of Bible teaching and preaching. This is a great presentation that anyone can understand and efficient for the great need of learning about Christ's soon return. This book will give successful answers to those who want to know. Dr. Hiltibidal is comprehensive in his preaching and teaching. He is my friend and I thank God for how He is using Dr. Hiltibidal in a mighty way through this great book.

Because He lives,

Dr. Randy Taylor
Evangelist

Acknowledgements

I want to thank my precious wife of 45 years for her labors of love in the ministry all these years. She has been such a blessing as a wife, mother, pastor's wife, musician, and typist.

She has helped make sense of what I have written all these years with her English skills. She has carefully examined and re-examined this little book, as she has most all my correspondence and lessons for public view all our lives together.

Other than the Lord Himself, any apparent success in my ministry is due to her faithfulness to the Lord and to me. She is a godly Proverbs 31 wife and mother, a true help meet from the Lord.

I want to thank Brother Ben Oats, a member of Grace Baptist Church of Bowling Green, Kentucky, for proofreading this manuscript. His love for the Lord and the ministry is evidenced by his many years of faithfulness and helping authors with checking and double checking their work with the skills in which the Lord has blessed him.

Table of Contents

Introduction — 1

Chapter One
Signs from the Olivet Discourse — 7

Chapter Two
Signs within Religion and the Church — 31

Chapter Three
The Romans One Syndrome — 52

Chapter Four
Babylonianism and the Endtimes — 68

Chapter Five
Daniel's Three Endtime Gods — 79

Chapter Six
The Battle of Psalms 83 — 91

Chapter Seven
Ezekiel 38 Allies and Outcome — 111

Conclusion — 131

About the Author — 136

Introduction to the Edge of Dawn

We live in interesting times as we are closing in on the final days of this age. People everywhere are speaking of our times and the events occurring around the world and wonder what it means.

There are those that, as the Scripture says, mock us who point to these as the last days. "And saying, Where is the promise of his coming? for since the fathers fell asleep, all things continue as they were from the beginning of the creation" (II Peter 3:4).

As I travel and speak in conferences and church services, I sense the uncertainty in the minds of far too many Christians concerning the times in which we live. Even lost people are sensing a change in the affairs of men that they cannot understand but to which they seek an answer.

I often hear this from preachers, "I have asked you to come to my church to speak on prophecy because I am not quite sure of these things but want my people to hear about them."

Of course, I find this hard to understand, but then I grew up in the 50s and 60s under the teaching ministry of my uncle who was known for his great insight and teaching concerning prophetic issues.

Most every preacher of the gospel has an area that seems to drive them into more study and mine has been in both science and the Bible and prophecy.

This work is by no means an in-depth study for there could be no end, so to speak, of the details available today of the signs of the times.

I simply desire to point out events occurring and changes taking place that point to the fact that we are coming to the end of this age, the Church Age in particular.

We will consider the teaching of our Lord in what we refer to as the Olivet Discourse, as He mentions the times of the Gentiles and a few of the signs indicating the end of that time, which I believe is fast approaching.

One of the problems of our times and a problem that has plagued Bible teaching throughout the Church Age is that we too often view prophecy through the lenses of our cultural glasses. By that I mean we too often try to fit our interpretations into our culture, seeing our times or geographical area as a center point instead of the Biblical center point.

This has produced many ideas concerning America's role in the endtimes or other nations as being of greater importance than the Scriptures really reveal.

Too often our nationalistic instincts override our spiritual insight, and this we must correct in order to properly understand prophecy.

Various philosophical ideas have developed over time that are not supported by Scripture or common sense. These must be refused in light of the truth of Scripture.

Replacement theology and dominion theology are neither supported by Scripture. Sure you can take a few verses and remove them from their context and support almost any philosophy or doctrine, but proper interpretation requires us to allow all Scripture to speak, and nothing will be correct if any Scripture refutes our idea. Following simple rules of interpretation will help us be correct in our understanding.

When it comes to prophecy, one key that is often overlooked is that the center point of prophecy is Israel and Jerusalem.

Too often the interpretations presented shift the center of prophetic emphasis from Israel to a focal point desired by the interpreter. As a result, many ideas and philosophies have been developed, such as Babylon in the endtimes is New York City, British Israelism, and others.

Often people ask why there is seemingly more interest today concerning this subject and the short answer is Israel.

From both the Old and New Testaments we find clear teaching that the final conclusion of the Gentile rule will take place when Israel is living as a nation of people in their own land.

From 70 AD until 1948 AD Israel was a scattered people among the nations of the world. Jesus stated this as a result of the Roman destruction of Jerusalem. Luke 21:24, "And they shall fall by the edge of the sword, and shall be led away captive into all nations: and Jerusalem shall be trodden down of the Gentiles, until the times of the Gentiles be fulfilled."

We will look at various signs from the Word of God that are evident in our times, all indicating the approaching tribulation and the end of Gentile rule.

As a futurist, pre-millennial, pre-tribulation rapturist, I see these signs as the stage being set for that Day of the Lord. They are not signs for the rapture, for there are no signs for that event; it has been eminent since the fall of Jerusalem in 70 AD.

We need to take serious our responsibility to the gospel with what time we have before the rapture or our personal appointment through death.

From the signs, the time between now and the start of the final countdown of seven years is growing shorter. I John 2:28, "And now, little children, abide in him; that, when he shall appear, we may have confidence, and not be ashamed before him at his coming."

We should see these times and the signs of what is coming not with fear but of excited anticipation of our soon departure from this world to meet our Saviour in the air and so shall we ever be!

A new day is fast approaching for planet earth, and the people left to face it will find it unbearable. As we see the signs of the approaching day, one cannot help but realize that we are at the edge of dawn.

Let us take the admonition the Apostle Paul gave to the believers at Ephesus. Ephesians 5:16, "Redeeming the time, because the days are evil." We need to make our time count while the opportunity is still before us, for we stand at the edge of the dawning of the Day of the Lord.

Chapter One

Signs from the Olivet Discourse

The Lord had been teaching the people a couple of days before the time of the Passover, and when He ended teaching in Matthew, Twenty-three, He left with His disciples to go across the valley to the Mount of Olives.

It appears that as they were departing through the temple grounds, they commented to Jesus concerning the great stones in the building of the temple. The temple had been under construction for many years and was not completed for many more years after this.

Josephus said some of these stones "were several stones which were forty-five cubits in length, five in height, and sixth in breadth;" that is more than seventy feet long, ten wide, and eight high.

Why they commented about them we do not know, but the Lord's reply must have startled them. "And Jesus said unto them, See ye not all these things? verily I say unto you, There shall not be left here one stone upon another, that shall not be thrown down" (Matthew 24:2).

Now we need to see the break in time from Verses Two and Three. They passed on through the temple area and then out the eastern wall down to the valley floor and a thousand or so yards to the hillside to the Mount of Olivet.

At least twenty or thirty minutes could easily have passed, and they were thinking about what He meant.

After they got seated, I suppose then they spoke up. Matthew 24:3, "And as he sat upon the mount of Olives, the disciples came unto him privately, saying, Tell us, when shall these things be? and what shall be the sign of thy coming, and of the end of the world?"

They asked Him three questions that He answered in the rest of the chapter. Though they asked three questions, they had them out of order, so the Lord answered them in the proper sequence. These are also covered in Mark 13:1-37 and Luke 21:6-38. A careful study of all three accounts will bring clear understanding of these three answers given by Jesus.

We will refrain from a deeper search into these questions, but focus on the signs that Jesus spoke of concerning the ending days of this age.

The Start of the End of this Age

I think it is important to see the statement of Jesus concerning a triggering of the start to the countdown of the Gentile rule. Before He made that statement, He set the stage of world affairs preceding this trigger. Matthew 24:6, "And ye shall hear of wars and rumours of wars: see that ye be not troubled: for all these things must come to pass, but the end is not yet."

There have been very few years in history with no wars, somewhere in the neighborhood of twenty or so years with relative peace. He said these regional conflicts and wars would continue throughout history but that when something different takes place we should take notice. Luke 21:10, "Then said he unto them, Nation shall rise against nation, and kingdom against kingdom."

Matthew adds a little more information to this. Matthew 24:7-8, "For nation shall rise against nation, and kingdom against kingdom: and there shall be famines, and pestilences, and earthquakes, in divers places. All these are the <u>beginning of sorrows</u>."

I believe this prophecy is in alignment with that of Ezekiel, Thirty-seven as the valley of dry bones pictures the revival of the nation of Israel for the final fulfillment of prophecy concerning Israel and the Gentile rule that has persecuted her through these centuries of time.

World War One was the first time in history where nations plural aligned themselves against other allied nations in war for control of the world. As a result of this war, a major shift began to take place in the world as a whole. Many things began to come together changing society, culture, politics, economics, education, and on and on.

The devil, it would appear, was setting up his run for control, but in reality it was God that was beginning to set the stage for the completion of His prophetic plan of the ages.

As a result of the First World War, what was called the Balfour Declaration sprang forward a movement that had already begun, known as Zionism, and launched it into full speed ahead.

The Jewish people began returning to the desolate land that had lain waste and for the most part empty of people. The Arab world and Palestinian sympathizers, including most Protestant and Catholic groups, tried to convince the world that the Jews stole the land from the Arab castoff, but this is far from the truth.

Keep in mind that these religious groups are the ones that claim a replacement theology and reject the current Israel as having any role in Biblical prophecy or any claims to God's promises made to the Israel of old.

As the valley of dry bones was gathering together, the world stage was shifting once again. The Second World War followed, which resulted in some very major changes in the landscape of the world. Nations were created and borders set by the League of Nations in the Middle East that are still points of great conflict.

May 17, 1948, Israel declared its sovereignty as Ezekiel's prophecy of the dry bones began to take flesh upon them. Immediately the enemies set out to destroy them, but God intervened. Several wars or conflicts later they are still oppressed and threatened by all their neighbors and are alone against the Gentile and Arab world.

A league of nations was developed after the Second World War to try to circumvent any further world wars in the future. This has morphed into the U.N.

These are all steps in guiding the world in these final days of this age toward a one world government.

The United States became the center stage of world affairs, especially by using our currency as the basis and stabilizer for world financial systems.

The Bretten Woods document was questioned and with good reason, and the world called for a new stabilizer or basis for world financial control.

It was the strength of this nation that provided a great gospel push in missionary outreach to the world that has ended up in a fulfillment of another of the Lord's prophecies concerning the church, which we will look at closer in the pages that follow.

As the churches of this nation grew more materialistic and false gospels were adapted to fit culture or the lost society, God's hand of blessing was removed.

Many changes took place on every level of society globally as a result of World War Two. A shift began to take place in all areas of cultural life that has resulted in the condition of societies worldwide at this time.

From that point forward the world has been headed towards the fulfillment of prophecy and the end of Gentile rule.

If we are not careful, we could grow discouraged at what has transpired, but may I remind you that this is God's doing and any part the evil one, Satan, has in it is by God's permission.

The world stage politically, militarily, economically, culturally, religiously, and many other areas indicate we stand at the edge of dawn.

The Beginning of Sorrows

Another key word in the Olivet Discourse is found in both Mark and Matthew, "the beginning of sorrows," meaning the pains of a woman in travail.

The picture that the Lord paints here is the process of a woman who is getting ready to deliver a child. After months of changes that are taken without a great deal of notice, all of a sudden one day something different happens. It's not just the usual kick of the feet but a definite change has happened.

It may last only a few moments and with little severe pain, but it is different. It is signaling that the beginning of the end has started. A few days may pass until the next episode, and it will be a little more in both intensity and duration.

These episodes continue to gain in intensity, frequency, and duration; this process continues until they culminate in the birth of the child.

The Lord uses this to illustrate that once the trigger point that starts the process takes place, there will be a continual process that will bring about the end of this age and the dawning of the Day of the Lord.

We have witnessed these past sixty years or so many changes in every area of life, each fulfilling its part in moving us along to the end of this age.

There has been much debate over certain prophecies, none any more so than that of the budding of the fig tree mentioned by Jesus.

Matthew 24:32-34, "Now learn a parable of the fig tree; When his branch is yet tender, and putteth forth leaves, ye know that summer is nigh: So likewise ye, when ye shall see all these things, know that it is near, even at the doors. Verily I say unto you, this generation shall not pass, till all these things be fulfilled."

How long is the generation? Some would say forty years, others seventy, and yet others one hundred. What appears to be a fact is that the culmination of this age will be during that time frame, whatever it is.

I would submit to your thinking that the term generation is not to be viewed so much as in so many years but the process involved from beginning to end, as the bud has a purpose to produce a flower and its purpose is to produce the fruit.

The Lord is speaking of the cycle from beginning to end being completed. Here it is in reference to Israel from its re-establishment to the start of the Millennial.

This includes the events of the endtimes and the seven years of tribulation.

We know that in 1948 Israel budded out and that springs forth another point of consideration, the starting point of the beginning of sorrows or was it the nations against nations? I prefer the latter since that seems to be the very words of our Lord. We could argue these points but for what!

The overwhelming evidence is that the trigger has been pulled, the hourglass has been turned up by the hand of God, and the clock is ticking towards the end of this age.

There are many that prefer to ignore the signs in hopes that they can continue to live their materialistic lives in a pseudo Christian way, but the end of this age is inevitable by God's decree.

So let us live in excited expectancy of the trump of God and the voice of the Archangel as the door of heaven is opened as seen by John as recorded in Revelation 4:1, "After this I looked, and, behold, a door was opened in heaven: and the first voice which I heard was as it were of a trumpet talking with me; which said, Come up hither, and I will shew thee things which must be hereafter."

Signs from Nature - Ecological Disasters

"...and there shall be famines, and pestilences, and earthquakes, in divers place" (Matthew 24:7b). Following the trigger that starts the beginning of the end, the Lord says there will be signs of the end seen in nature.

Don't you just get sick of the meteorologists and New Age people speaking of "Mother Nature"? It is Father God they had better be considering instead of ignoring the signs.

But it was the Lord that told us in His conversation with Nicodemus that the lost person cannot see the things of God.

They see the signs and through their Pantheistic mindset blame it on global warming. They see this as caused by man and to a certain extent it is the result of man's doing since it is related to the results of sin that has infected the earth.

What they cannot see, due to the blindness of their own lost nature, is that though they think they are moving the world towards a better future, it is God that is moving his agenda down the road to the end of this age.

As we approach the edge of dawn, we see the blindness of not only society but that of the so-called

Christian to the signs that were foretold by the Lord himself.

These are not only signs of the impending day that is fast approaching but are judgments upon the wickedness of man and the Gentile treatment of God's people and His land Israel.

Famines

Warnings are posted daily by world organizations concerning the food supply of the world. As of this writing, the world is set on a course for famine.

UN Warns Of Looming Worldwide Food Crisis In 2013

--World grain reserves are so dangerously low that severe weather in the United States or other food-exporting countries could trigger a major hunger crisis next year, the United Nations has warned.

--Failing harvests in the US, Ukraine and other countries this year have eroded reserves to their lowest level since 1974. The US, which has experienced record heat waves and droughts in 2012, now holds in reserve a historically low 6.5%

of the maize that it expects to consume in the next year, says the UN.

--With food consumption exceeding the amount grown for six of the past 11 years, countries have run down reserves from an average of 107 days of consumption 10 years ago to under 74 days recently.

--Prices of main food crops such as wheat and maize are now close to those that sparked riots in 25 countries in 2008. FAO figures released this week suggest that 870 million people are malnourished and the food crisis is growing in the Middle East and Africa. Wheat production this year is expected to be 5.2% below 2011, with yields of most other crops, except rice, also falling, says the UN.

The reports of impending disasters of food production and the added use of staple crops for conversion into petroleum products have the world on the edge of famine.

Some would say this is the black horse of the apocalypse, but it is not, for that cannot ride until after the first two horsemen. They will not ride until the Antichrist is revealed and that cannot occur until after the rapture of the believers according to II Thessalonians, Chapter Two.

What we are seeing is the foreshadowing of ominous things to come and cannot even be compared to the future famine that is seen in the early days of the tribulation.

An example of the coming famine and its results can be seen in the story of Joseph and Pharaoh found in Genesis. At the end of the first three and one-half years everything was under the total control of the government.

Genesis 47:13-21, "And there was no bread in all the land; for the famine was very sore, so that the land of Egypt and all the land of Canaan fainted by reason of the famine. And Joseph gathered up all the money that was found in the land of Egypt, and in the land of Canaan, for the corn which they bought: and Joseph brought the money into Pharaoh's house. And when money failed in the land of Egypt, and in the land of Canaan, all the Egyptians came unto Joseph, and said, Give us bread: for why should we die in thy presence? for the money faileth. And Joseph said, Give your cattle; and I will give you for your cattle, if money fail. And they brought their cattle unto Joseph: and Joseph gave them bread in exchange for horses, and for the flocks, and for the cattle of the herds, and for the asses: and he fed them with bread for all their cattle for that year. When that year was ended, they came unto him the second year, and said unto him, We will not hide it from my lord, how that our money is spent; my lord also hath our herds of cattle; there is not ought left in the sight of my lord, but our bodies, and our lands: Wherefore shall we die before thine eyes, both we and our land? buy us and our land for bread, and we and our land will be servants unto Pharaoh: and give us seed, that we may live, and not die, that the land be not desolate. And Joseph bought all the land of Egypt for Pharaoh; for the Egyptians sold every man his field, because the famine prevailed over them: so the land became Pharaoh's. And as for the people, he removed them to cities from one end of the borders of Egypt even to the other end thereof."

It appears that history could repeat itself and by the middle of the tribulation period, the Antichrist could take complete control just as prophecy has declared.

Every day's news reveals signs of famine around the globe and the forecast of very serious times ahead.

The prophecy of Revelation, Chapter Six would indicate the result of the first two riders will produce great famine, which is pictured by the third or black horse. The natural result of war is the devastation of land and the scarcity of food.

Jesus said that though we see this sign, the end is not yet--that is the end of this age. "For all these things must come to pass, but the end is not yet" (Matthew 24:6b).

Pestilences

Pestilences mean an epidemic of disease, a highly contagious or infectious disease, or a series of infectious diseases. History records times of pestilences resulting in huge numbers of fatalities. But since the trigger that has started the countdown to the end of this age, there has been both advances in antibiotics and vaccines to fight disease and an increasing antibiotic resistant strain of viruses come about.

Headline 10-22-12

The Armageddon Virus: Experts Fear A Disease That Leaps From Animals To Humans Could Devastate Mankind In The Next Five Years

> *--The symptoms appear suddenly with a headache, high fever, joint pain, stomach pain and vomiting. As the illness progresses, patients can develop large areas of bruising and uncontrolled bleeding. In at least 30 per cent of cases, Crimean-Congo Viral Hemorrhagic Fever is fatal.*
>
> *And so it proved this month when a 38-year-old garage owner from Glasgow, who had been to his brother's wedding in Afghanistan, became the*

UK's first confirmed victim of the tick-borne viral illness when he died at the high-security infectious disease unit at London's Royal Free Hospital.

It is a disease widespread in domestic and wild animals in Africa and Asia — and one that has jumped the species barrier to infect humans with deadly effect.

But the unnamed man's death was not the only time recently a foreign virus had struck in this country for the first time. Last month, a 49-year-old man entered London's St. Thomas' Hospital with a raging fever, severe cough and desperate difficulty in breathing.

He bore all the hallmarks of the deadly Sars virus that killed nearly 1,000 people in 2003 — but blood tests quickly showed that this terrifyingly virulent infection was not Sars. Nor was it any other virus yet known to medical science.

The reports from news sources daily indicate that humanity stands at the brink of disease outbreaks with no antibodies to fight them off.

Almost daily reports are given of diseases that are mutating and with no foreseen cure or remedy in sight.

Add to this the manipulation of viruses by pharmaceutical companies to produce serums of vaccines that are not regulated nearly as well as you might think. And who knows but what for the sake of financial gain devious evil minded humanity might do!

Add to this mix the chemical and biological weapons that are ready for use against humanity and the increase of pestilences is inevitable.

We can assume that these will be seen in great force as the fourth and pale rider rides in the early part of the tribulation. The result of those days is seen in Revelation 6:8, "And I looked, and behold a pale horse: and his name that sat on him was Death, and Hell followed with him. And power was given unto them over the fourth part of the earth, to kill with sword, and with hunger, and with death, and with the beasts of the earth."

One-fourth of the earth's population will die in the first few months to three years of the tribulation.

Jesus said that we would see an increase in these things before that day comes, and we are at the edge of dawn for such things.

Earthquakes in Divers Places

There is not a day that passes without the report of numerous earthquakes around the world. Some would say there have always been earthquakes and that we just have a better system of discovery and reporting.

This is true, but there does appear to be an overall increase, as well as the number that measures five or above on the Richter scale. With the access through the computer world, real time accounts are easily attained and it is obvious that there is an increase.

At the time of this writing there have been fifty earthquakes at 5.3 to 7.2 take place in the past twelve days.

The chain of volcanic and seismic platelet shifts called the "ring of fire" that encircles the oceans has some trembling in it every day. Volcanologists are predicting that a course is set for an eventual cataclysmic eruption that will send the earth into darkness and all sorts of tragedy.

Just as the stage is being set politically, socially, and religiously for the final seven years of God's divine judgment, a gradual changing unnoticed by many also is the physical earth being prepared for the final judgment of God.

Revelation 16:17-21, "And the seventh angel poured out his vial into the air; and there came a great voice out of the temple of heaven, from the throne, saying, It is done. And there were voices, and thunders, and lightnings; and there was a great earthquake, such as was not since men were upon the earth, so mighty an earthquake, and so great. And the great city was divided into three parts, and the cities of the nations fell: and great Babylon came in remembrance before God, to give unto her the cup of the wine of the fierceness of his wrath. And every island fled away, and the mountains were not found. And there fell upon men a great hail out of heaven, every stone about the weight of a talent: and men blasphemed God because of the plague of the hail; for the plague thereof was exceeding great."

The seventh and final plague that ends the tribulation and brings the presence of the Lord at Armageddon is the greatest earthquake that has ever taken place. It results in the islands disappearing, the mountains being brought down, and the cities destroyed as God reshapes and prepares to remake a world for the Millennial Reign.

It would appear from many Scriptures that for that one thousand years' time the earth will be restored to a similar condition as it was before the flood. The topography, the nature of the animal world, and the healthy long life of humanity are but a few of the things prophesied concerning this time to come.

The present global earthquake phenomena is simply the stage being set in the geology of the earth, waiting for the voice of God to speak at that fateful moment at the end of the Day of the Lord.

Signs in the Heavens

Luke 21:11, "And great earthquakes shall be in divers places, and famines, and pestilences; and fearful sights and great signs shall there be from heaven."

Astronomy and astrology are not one and the same.

Astronomers, with the aid of scientific advances and space exploration, are constantly finding new discoveries, often discoveries of great distress and concern.

The study of the stars and the universe is an undeniable statement of the omniscience and omnipotence of our Creator, God.

The more we learn about the heavens the more we realize how little we know. Truly the Scripture is true. Isaiah 55:9, "For as the heavens are higher than the earth, so are my ways higher than your ways, and my thoughts than your thoughts."

Psalms 8:3, "When I consider thy heavens, the work of thy fingers, the moon and the stars, which thou hast ordained."

The names of hundreds of millions or billions of stars in millions or billions of galaxies are known by their Creator as the heavens sheweth forth His handiwork. Psalms 147:4, "He telleth the number of the stars; he calleth them all by their names."

Is it not striking that in the Genesis account of creation on day number four, after the Lord places the sun and moon in their orbits, that He says in Genesis 1:16, "And God made two great lights; the greater light to rule the day, and the lesser light to rule the night: he made the stars also." As if to say, "Oh by the way, I made the stars also."

The devil long ago took the stars and the alignment of planets and star groups and distorted them for his use to deceive the world with astrology. No Christian should have anything to do with this tool of the devil.

An Article in the Christian Worldview and Issues 10-25-13

More Brits Believe In Aliens Than In God, Survey Claims

--The number of those who believe in extraterrestrial life is significantly higher than

those who believe in God in the United Kingdom, a new survey claims.

The Bible tells us that from the start God placed the bodies in the heavens with a purpose. That purpose was for the present time and a time to come.

Genesis 1:14, "And God said, Let there be lights in the firmament of the heaven to divide the day from the night; and let them be for signs, and for seasons, and for days, and years."

Just as from the beginning He designed the star movements that signaled the birth of the Saviour, He has designed the timing of events yet to come.

Just this past year, a comet or asteroid passed closer to us than the sun as it passed between us. That has never before happened. This happened at the same time the geo-polar alignment took place between the earth, the moon, and the sun.

Much speculation resulted. It is thought that this and a similar one caused the magnetic pull on earth platelets that resulted in the earthquake in Japan, which moved that whole Island eight feet from its original geographical position.

During the tribulation there will be many signs in the heavens; even the sun and moon will give only partial light after the sun has burned so brightly that men are scorched by its heat.

We are witnessing an amazing level of solar flares that are emitting enormous energy influxes. This could affect our weather and increase severe storms as well as interfere with satellite communications and the electric grid system that affect life on the entire planet.

As Christians, we need not worry; we just need to keep our ears ready to hear the shout to come up hither and our minds on the winning of souls for Christ.

The signs from the Olivet Discourse, just as Jesus foretold, are being seen, and we can know that we stand at the edge of dawn.

Chapter Two

Signs within Religion and the Church

Jesus gave us some signs in His discourse on the Church Age in the parables of Matthew, Chapter Thirteen. There He gives a prophetic overview of the church from its inception by Him personally and to its final end at the rapture.

Within this overview, He covers several issues that we could call signs pointing to the end of the age. Before we examine that, let's set the foundation as set forth by the Lord in these eight parables.

These parables should be seen as a unit, each relating to the other with a consistent interpretation to each symbol used. Too often preachers and commentators fail to follow proper rules for interpretation. This is why I wrote the book entitled **All the Parables of Matthew Thirteen**, *Jesus' prophetic teaching concerning the Church Age.*

Let me again state some principles that should be followed when seeking a proper understanding of the parables, as well as any portion of Scripture.

Principles of Interpretation

1. Everyone and everything in the story is symbolic of something else. The symbol used is not to be taken literally for it is being used symbolically of a literal event, action, attitude, person, etc. It may be a literal object but is being used symbolically. (Old bottles and new wine were literal, but they were used symbolically of the New Testament and Old Testament with the Jewish law and ceremonies.) "Neither do men put new wine into old bottles: else the bottles break, and the wine runneth out, and the bottles perish: but they put new wine into new bottles, and both are preserved" (Matthew 9:17).

2. The key that unlocks the symbolism is found either within the context or elsewhere in Scripture.

Knowing the context of the parable is all so important. Often people try to understand or make references to certain Scriptures outside of their context and may believe or teach an erroneous doctrine.

One must always keep a text within its context and remember that Scripture never contradicts itself. So, if your belief or teaching is based on a single or few verses, yet there are other verses that do not agree, then it is your belief that is wrong and not the Scripture.

No one has the authority to manipulate Scripture and no Scripture is of any private interpretation.

The principle of first mention should apply to all Scripture including parables. The meaning or interpretation never changes from its first mention, including the effects associated with the first mention.

3. There are three guidelines in interpreting parables: context, Scripture, and expositional constancy.

In the Bible, things used symbolically in one place are generally used in the same way throughout. Leaven (or yeast) always symbolizes sin. Adultery and fornication always symbolize the worship of other gods, a spiritual unfaithfulness.

This is what is meant by the principle of expositional constancy, consistently using the same symbolism with the same meaning.

There are those who use other forms of interpretation so that they change the meaning of symbolism to promote their own ideas or views, claiming that Scripture supports their interpretation.

Observing these guidelines will help you correctly interpret parables and increase your overall knowledge of Scripture at the same time.

Parable One:
The Sower and the Seed

In this first parable we can understand that it was Jesus Christ Himself that initiates the church and what we have come to call the Church Age.

The seed is the gospel, which is simply the account of the death, burial, and resurrection of Jesus. A person must believe this as truth and place their faith or complete trust and reliance in the promise that God will save them, if they will accept His offer of eternal life based on the redemption provided on Calvary's cross.

Today the gospel has become polluted and unclear by the compromise of religious leaders. Social and cultural issues have evolved, and sadly too many religious leaders have allowed an evolving of the gospel they now present to satisfy the world, rather than adhere to the Biblical account of the gospel.

The gospel is simple and has not changed because the Lord and His Word have not changed. I Corinthians 15:3-4, "For I delivered unto you first of all that which I also received, how that Christ died for our sins according to the scriptures; And that he was buried, and that he rose again the third day according to the scriptures."

It is in this first parable that the Lord informs us that of the four types of hearts referred to as soil; only one seems to respond properly in order to produce fruit.

From the next parable we see that it is the sons of God, those born again, that the church is built upon, or as Jesus said to Peter, it was his confession of faith that is the rock and foundation of the church.

We will refrain from too lengthy a discussion here, but I believe from Scripture there is no such thing as a universal or invisible church but local assemblies.

That assembly is to be made up of truly born again believers that have been scripturally baptized by the proper authority, who can form a called out assembly for the purpose of fulfilling the great commission given to the church and through the church to each member of that church.

The Result of Fruitfulness

Within this first parable, the Lord gives us a sign that in a general way describes the Church Age from the start to its final days. Matthew 13:8, "But other fell into good ground, and brought forth fruit, some an hundredfold, some sixtyfold, some thirtyfold."

It appears that at its beginning the results were phenomenal with multitudes receiving the gospel. This continued for a few centuries even with tens of thousands yea millions martyred for their faith. It began with a hundred fold yield, but along the way, due to the effects of what Jesus will explain in following parables, that yield went down to sixty fold.

By the end of the Church Age, it will be reduced to a thirty fold yield. If you think that true Christianity is seriously lived by today's "Christian world" as in its early days, then you may as well put this book down now, for you are too blind to see the truth that faces you every day.

In this first parable, Jesus gives a general statement concerning the process through time that the church would pass. No wonder He said in Luke 18:8b, "Nevertheless when the Son of man cometh, shall he find faith on the earth?"

Parable Two:
The Tares among the Wheat

An enemy came along and planted a look alike but one that had no life to produce. That enemy was the devil, and from the start he began trying to attack the gospel by various ways and means.

These were to be left until the end of this age. Then God will take care of correcting it.

We may as well come to the understanding that the false teachers and the spreaders of false doctrine will haunt the church now as it has always done.

Do not get caught up in studying the false doctrine so as to understand in order to argue. No! But study the Word so as to know the truth and simply proclaim the truth realizing multitudes will prefer doctrines of devils over truth.

If your taste buds are used to the taste of good food, one bite of that which is bad is immediately recognized and spit out. So train your spiritual taste on truth and when error is brought to you, you will immediately recognize it to be bad.

Paul had to deal with these tares as they were teaching justification by adhering to the law. He even had to confront Peter about these issues and they came back to the Scriptures and faith alone. Paul wrote many letters about this issue that is preserved in your Bible.

As time progressed this became more and more of a problem as false doctrine of all sorts was introduced, including the altering of Holy Scripture in the first century.

In the following parables, he will further explain the process that reduces the fruitfulness of the Church Age.

Parable Three: The Mustard Seed

This parable goes back to the first and paints another picture of this change in fruitfulness. Here he uses an illustration that is plain to see to illustrate the change in nature that will occur during the Church Age.

Matthew 13:31-32, "Another parable put he forth unto them, saying, The kingdom of heaven is like to a grain of mustard seed, which a man took, and sowed in his field: Which indeed is the least of all seeds: but when it is grown, it is the greatest among herbs, and becometh a tree, so that the birds of the air come and lodge in the branches thereof."

We now will see the signs Jesus spoke of concerning the ending days of the Church Age. But first notice the change of nature that takes place within that time.

And Becometh a Tree

The seed used to represent the beginning of the church is a mustard seed or plant. While it is true this plant does indeed grow tall and small birds can rest in its branches, it is not the point that we need to understand.

It is that which began as an herb that becomes a deciduous tree. A change in nature is what Jesus is pointing out.
This change that has taken place is the result of the tares, and Jesus will explain how that was done in the next parable.

What is seen in our times as perceived Christianity is not Biblical Christianity at all. The vast majority of people that claim to be Christians are not even born again and have no claim to the gospel.

The nature has changed, but there are still some true Bible believing churches and Christians. God always has his remnant of true followers.

True Christian people, whose calling, hope, citizenship, and destiny are heavenly, are not rooted as a tree into this present world.

That which is represented by this "tree" is not a people who are "strangers and pilgrims" down here, but a system whose roots lie deeply in this present world, which aims at greatness and expansion.

You could discuss as to when this nature change came about, but it appears that by the late third and early fourth centuries a major change had taken place.

The marriage of politics and religion adopting all sorts of pagan and satanic festivals and holy days were

"Christianized" and paganism became accepted as Christianity.

The Birds of the Air Come and Lodge in the Branches

Birds are always symbolic of the workers of the evil one, the tares that lodge or make their abode in the overspreading of the endtime church.

The "birds" lodging in the branches of this tree make this impossible to teach that the gospel will overflow and Christianity will rule the world.

If Scripture be compared with Scripture, it will be found that these "birds" symbolize Satan's agents. In Verse 4, the word used is "fowls", "and the fowls came and devoured them up."

In Genesis 15:11, we are told that the "fowls came down upon the carcasses" (the bodies of the sacrifices) and that "Abram drove them away." Here, beyond doubt, they prefigure the efforts of Satan to render null and void the sacrifice of the Lord Jesus.

It seems that Jesus is saying one of the signs of the endtimes is the overwhelming control of evil unsaved leaders in perceived Christianity.

It appears that as the Church Age draws to a close that the birds in the branches of its religious influence will overshadow the world.

Today, like never before, all sorts of "Christian leaders" are working feverishly to form a religion that has some sort of Christian flavor that is acceptable to the vast multitudes of the world.

Is this not what other portions of Scripture tell us will happen as the world is being prepared for the Day of the Lord!

We need to see the fourth parable and the picture will become much clearer as the signs in the church or religion called Christianity are evident.

Parable Four: The Leaven

Matthew 13: 33, "Another parable spake he unto them; The kingdom of heaven is like unto leaven, which a woman took, and hid in three measures of meal, till the whole was leavened."

This has nothing to do with a person's salvation like the Calvinist would have you believe. We must follow the rules established for interpretation. Leaven always represents sin, not the gospel.

This has to do with the process the tares used to bring about the change within Christianity's nature.

Calvinists understand the "three measures of meal" to represent God's elect, and hidden inside of every person is divine truth, and at some point they will be awakened to discover its presence and respond in becoming a believer.

But if "leaven" is the symbol of corrupting evil, and the meal stands for the pure truth of God, then this parable also supplies a picture of Christianity as a whole, and that ultimately the gospel or the truth of God is to be corrupted throughout Christendom.

The "leaven" symbolizes the corrupting of God's truth by the introduction of evil doctrine. Compare Matthew 16:12, "Then understood they how that he bade them not beware of the leaven of bread, but of the doctrine of the Pharisees and of the Sadducees."

What we have witnessed over the past century is a major shift in what churches see as their purpose and the message they present.

The pursuit of materialism has caused many to adapt the gospel to a way to gain wealth, while others look for eternal life in this body and have designed a gospel of physical health.

Pole driven ministries have caused them to change the gospel from that which confronts the sinner with their need of salvation to one that accommodates the sinner and makes them feel comfortable in the modern church service.

One of the signs of the times is the change taking place in what is seen as Christianity today. The evolving movement called the emergent church is developing into that pictured by the Lord as an overspreading of the earth.

Those of us that stay by the truth unchanged by society and culture are few compared to the greater majority that goes by the name of Christian.

Our voice is unheard by the world at large, but the voices of the movers and shakers of the emergent church movement, along with the leaders of various forms of so-called Christianity, are heard around the world.

The leaven of false doctrine promoted by these so-called leaders has set a course for a universal global worldwide accepted religion. The final phase of this modern movement will no doubt be the one the false prophet, the second beast of Revelation 13:11, will direct for the Antichrist worship of the tribulation.

This has caused a great apostasy to begin that we are told would be a sign of the endtimes.

II Thessalonians 2:3, "Let no man deceive you by any means: for that day shall not come, except there come a falling away first, and that man of sin be revealed, the son of perdition."

II Timothy 4:3-4, "For the time will come when they will not endure sound doctrine; but after their own lusts shall they heap to themselves teachers, having itching ears; And they shall turn away their ears from the truth, and shall be turned unto fables."

The work of the tares with their leaven has produced great change in Christianity. When we left the Philadelphian era and moved into the Laodicean time at the beginning of the twentieth century, there were many various movements within Christianity, all by the name of church.

At the closing of the Philadelphian age, the tares were at work tampering with the Word of God. They had discovered the early work of first and third century tares that had altered and changed many of the manuscripts of their day.

Having the same spirit as the previous tares, they set out to change Christianity for the future.

Studies and materials of this effort and its advancement are available to us, so I will not go into any depth on this matter for that is not the purpose of this work.

Sufficient is the evidence of the change they have produced in modern Christianity. Since the turn of the twentieth century, various versions of the Bible have come about until there seems to be one for the acceptance of everyone, even though they are lost and live lives in direct opposition to God's truth.

Along with this changing of God's Word, numerous religious movements have come about with various names except church. The doctrines of the greater majority of these are at odds with the truth of God's Word. Their practices and beliefs are more often than not strange and foreign to the Bible yet have become accepted by the majority who go by the name of Christ.

If the apostles, or for that fact the generation living at the end of the Philadelphian era, were to visit these churches, they would not recognize them as Christian.

The work of the tare with the use of their leaven has brought great changes in the nature of Christianity, and what Jesus prophesied through these parables has come to pass.

The Universal Endtime Religion

The evolving church movements of our times are a sign of the end days.

Daily the news comes from all over the world of the merging movements blending the various religions of the world ever closer to an accepted form of religion, uniting a world in a religion acceptable for all.

This seems to be what is pictured in the overspreading branches of the endtime church. Thank the Lord for the churches, pastors, and peoples of God that refuse to be removed from the narrow way that leads to life everlasting.

The only hold back to a perfect utopian religious world conceived in the hearts of the emergent church crowd is those of us that are sealed and possessed of the Holy Spirit. If they could just quiet our voice of opposition to their deceptive actions, they could attain their objective of a one world religion.

Sadly, the numbers of resistance to their goals is dwindling as the devil, the master deceiver, is working on those that still hold to the truth, and little by little he is capturing them with his tricks bringing them to compromise.

They refuse to compromise with their Bible, and they refuse to compromise with their doctrine, so he finds a common point that builds a bridge between the two views or the two sides of Christianity.

Music

What the devil could not do with the altering of the Word of God and with emotionalism and health and wealth gospels he has begun to accomplish through the medium of music.

As the former choir director of heaven's angelic choir, he understands the power and the use of music. He knows the innate instinct of humanity and how it responds to the effects of music on both the body and soul of man.

With the aid of music, he has been able to do what he could never have accomplished by any other means.

Multitudes of once sound in doctrine churches have through the influence of music been converted into progressive and liberal leaning religious movements, who have taken the name church or Baptist off their names.

More apostate movements are brought together and expanded through music than any other tool in the devil's arsenal.

Contemporary Christian music has destroyed more fundamental churches than any new version of the Bible or heresy and false doctrine could have ever accomplished.

Again, much could be said here, but it is not the purpose of this work. I simply desire to point out the dangers of starting down the road of compromise provided by contemporary Christian music.

Actually, that seems to be an oxymoron for true Christianity is the same as it has always been and contemporary seems to indicate a change needed to bring something from the past up to the current times, customs, and ways of doing things.

The change that is needed is not to bring Christianity down to an acceptable standard for the world but to hold it high and bring people up to God's standard.

This seems to be the exact purpose of the new music being used in so many churches today. They are on the road to compromise without seeing it.

For the music being used is from people of impure doctrine, unsound testimonies of salvation, and ties to Mysticism, among other problems; therefore the leaven is ever so slyly slipped in and change begins to take place.

Before long the leaders and people want to change practices and beliefs to match the new music and before you realize it another church has fallen away to fables.

The best cure is to never start down that road in the first place. "Well, we can't get the crowds to come and after all, if we can't get them in, we can't preach the gospel!"

Whatever happened to following the Bible in going out into the highways and byways and compelling them to come in!

Why have we adopted the world's idea of what constitutes success? The church is to be a peculiar people, a called-out assembly of born again believers. You can have a crowd and not have a church. God's description of success is not the number of people but the faithfulness of the people. The endtime apostasy we see today is one of the greatest signs that we are living in the endtimes.

The purpose of the church is not earthly but heavenly.

With these changes has come also a change in the purpose of the church. Most programs of today's religious movements are social and cultural in nature rather than eternal.

The great commission is still God's purpose for the church, and those that live and breathe for that singular purpose are still blessed of the Lord.

Success is not so much measured in numbers or a crowd but the striving to be faithful to the purpose and heartbeat of God, the worldwide spreading of the gospel.

Chapter Three

The Romans One Syndrome

"Because that, when they knew God, they glorified him not as God, neither were thankful; but became vain in their imaginations, and their foolish heart was darkened. Professing themselves to be wise, they became fools, And changed the glory of the uncorruptible God into an image made like to corruptible man, and to birds, and fourfooted beasts, and creeping things. Wherefore God also gave them up to uncleanness through the lusts of their own hearts, to dishonour their own bodies between themselves: Who changed the truth of God into a lie, and worshipped and served the creature more than the Creator, who is blessed for ever. Amen. For this cause God gave them up unto vile affections: for even their women did change the natural use into that which is against nature: And likewise also the men, leaving the natural use of the woman, burned in their lust one toward another; men with men working that which is unseemly, and receiving in themselves that recompence of their error which was meet. And even as they did not like to retain God in their knowledge, God gave them over to a reprobate mind, to do those things which are not convenient; Being filled with all unrighteousness, fornication, wickedness, covetousness, maliciousness; full of envy, murder, debate, deceit, malignity; whisperers,

Backbiters, haters of God, despiteful, proud, boasters, inventors of evil things, disobedient to parents, Without understanding, covenantbreakers, without natural affection, implacable, unmerciful: Who knowing the judgment of God, that they which commit such things are worthy of death, not only do the same, but have pleasure in them that do them" (Romans 1:21-32).

We certainly are living in times that fit the description given to us in these verses. The saddest part of this is that it is not only the lost heathen crowd that fit the description but all too many that claim the name of Christ.

This may fit under the previous chapter and the apostasy of the church, but I place it here because it is a sign of the endtimes in its overall scenario.

The moral denigration taking place in the world today is not limited to the pagans and heathens only but to the religious movements as well.

A Failure to Recognize God in All Things

"Because that, when they knew God, they glorified him not as God, neither were thankful; but became vain in their imaginations, and their foolish heart was darkened."

Many pages of commentary could be penned concerning these few verses. But suffice it to say, all one need to do is look around at the present world to see its description is of our times.

All ages have had a great deal of this diluted thinking and living, but as time for the Church Age runs out and the less effect Christianity has on the world, the more this type of culture will grow.

The overall religious movements that were under the umbrella of Christianity have for centuries stood in opposition to the ungodliness described in these verses, but that has abruptly changed.

With the apostatizing of the church has come an acceptance of a wicked lifestyle both without and within the church. God's people once were known for their separated living but no longer.

Materialism has eaten up humanity until our own lives and our churches have become acceptable of the changes in culture and society as a whole.

The humanism of the Babylonian world system has now come into far too many churches until the Romans One Syndrome has become a part of it along with the world.

Vain in their imaginations and foolish in their heart well describes both the world and most of Christianity in our times.

Wise Fools

"Professing themselves to be wise, they became fools."

We have become so wise in our own understanding that we have come up with new and better ways with which to do church than God ever thought. New music, new methods, new programs, new Bibles, new you name it, and we wonder why the influence of modern day Christianity has little to no effect on culture.

Could it be we have allowed culture to affect us until we are irrelevant to both the world and our God?

It was in the middle of the last century that we in this nation caught up with the European nations in our turning our back completely on God. The pseudo-science of evolution took full control of the educational institutions and now with no thought to the God of creation a culture has been educated in that false religion. "Who changed the truth of God into a lie, and worshipped and served the creature more than the Creator."

Immoral Society and Church

As a result, society has been turned over "to uncleanness through the lusts of their own hearts" and all forms of immorality have become accepted in today's culture "to dishonour their own bodies between themselves."

This has brought us to the next phase. "For this cause God gave them up unto vile affections: for even their women did change the natural use into that which is against nature: And likewise also the men, leaving the natural use of the woman, burned in their lust one toward another; men with men working that which is unseemly, and receiving in themselves that recompence of their error which was meet."

Is this not the society we now live in? We who would dare speak against such sin are the outcast and condemned! "Who changed the truth of God into a lie." This is to be expected of the heathen pagans of the world, but this has become the norm for so-called "Christianity."

From mainline churches to the emergent crowd and even those that would go by the name Baptist are in this category.

A Totally Debased World

From "uncleanness through the lusts of their own hearts, unto vile affections," then to a reprobate mind, "to do those things which are not convenient."

We now live in the final stage where it says, "Who knowing the judgment of God, that they which commit such things are worthy of death, not only do the same, but have pleasure in them that do them."

Justice is almost unheard of today as tolerance has blinded the mind to truth. The false religions are given free rein in society from the education centers of indoctrination, to the business boardroom, to the political centers of government, and to the judge's chambers.

We are where Israel stood as they were ready for the judgment of God for their great sin as recorded in Isaiah 59:14, "And judgment is turned away backward, and justice standeth afar off: for truth is fallen in the street, and equity cannot enter."

This once great nation built upon Biblical foundations with a constitutional government is being turned inside out by the process of the Romans Chapter One Syndrome.

The Darkness of a Nation and Religion

The churches that once preached against sin and gave the gospel and saw cities and villages transformed are almost a thing of the past. Those that still declare "thus sayeth the Lord" are seen as odd and out of touch with reality when it is the outsider that is living outside of reality.

The darkness of the world is getting darker partly because the light from those responsible for shining it into the darkness fail in their responsibility.

Luke 11:34-35, "The light of the body is the eye: therefore when thine eye is single, thy whole body also is full of light; but when thine eye is evil, thy body also is full of darkness. Take heed therefore that the light which is in thee be not darkness."

This blindness, coupled with arrogance, has brought us to reject truth, rebel against truth, and now declare war on the truth. The very institution that is responsible for correcting and setting the true course, the church, is so far off course it can't find its own way back to God, let alone guide others.

The condition of modern Christianity is like the religious leaders of Jesus' earthly ministry. Luke 6:39, "And he spake a parable unto them, Can the blind lead the blind? shall they not both fall into the ditch?"

Sadly, the Romans One Syndrome has crippled the one institution and the only institution with the only remedy for the problems of society, the church.

Let us not be weary lest we faint, for unless, we the true children of God break out of this syndrome, what hope is there! I Peter 4:17, "For the time is come that judgment must begin at the house of God: and if it first begin at us, what shall the end be of them that obey not the gospel of God?"

We may never see revival on a national level, but we can experience it in our own hearts and lives, our own churches, in our area of ministry, but it will require us, the people of God, to be usable in His service.

It would appear that as a nation we have crossed a threshold of no return, as it seems that war against God is in force from the top to the bottom of our land.

Unlike the nation of Nineveh when Jonah preached repentance or perish and they repented and were spared, we are more like Nineveh years later when Nahum preached certain judgment with no hope of repentance to avert God's impending judgment.

The difference between the two responses to the Word of the Lord and the two endings is repentance.

When Jonah preached, they called for repentance from top to bottom. Jonah 3:5-7, "So the people of Nineveh believed God, and proclaimed a fast, and put on sackcloth, from the greatest of them even to the least of them. For word came unto the king of Nineveh, and he arose from his throne, and he laid his robe from him, and covered him with sackcloth, and sat in ashes. And he caused it to be proclaimed and published through Nineveh by the decree of the king and his nobles, saying, Let neither man nor beast, herd nor flock, taste any thing: let them not feed, nor drink water."

I do not sense in any form this to be the attitude of our land except within the few true churches and Christians who desire a genuine walk with their Lord.

The reason that Nahum's message was so intense and without hope was that Nineveh had now declared war against God. For that they could repent and plead for mercy, but still nothing would remove certain judgment. The line had been crossed and judgment was sure.

Has America gone too far is a question of great importance. From all appearances it would seem so, and if that is the case, the end of the Romans One Syndrome is destruction and judgment.

The last word of the burden of Nineveh from the pen of Nahum sums it up.

Nahum 3:19, "There is no healing of thy bruise; thy wound is grievous: all that hear the bruit of thee shall clap the hands over thee: for upon whom hath not thy wickedness passed continually?"

The Home under Attack

The Psalmist said this of a nation in Psalms 11:3, "If the foundations be destroyed, what can the righteous do?"

The foundation of any society is its families and the Romans One Syndrome has taken a great toll on the family.

Many factors have come into play against the homes in our nation and sadly they have devastated the Christian homes as equally as they have the pagans around us.

The re-defining of the family unit is a blatant attack against God and His original design for the home. The allowance of same sex marriages is an abomination and great sin, one from which the judgment of God will not be stayed. "For even their women did change the natural use into that which is against nature: And likewise also the men, leaving the natural use of the woman, burned in their lust one toward another; men with men working that which is unseemly, and receiving in themselves that recompence of their error which was meet."

The shame being placed on not only this nation but the greater number of the nations of the world by this grave sin is a stench reaching the very throne of God.

This is compounded with the statement concerning the women changing and going against what is natural – this would include the abortion of their unborn children – and places us and the nations of the world in great jeopardy of the judgment of God even if we tried to repent, though that looks unlikely.

The educational system of our day has become an indoctrination station, preparing the minds of the future with perverse living seen as right, and what the Bible instructs as right is now seen as the evil.

The elite, or so they think themselves to be, want a society that will serve them and be dependent upon their leaders so that no one will desire to place themselves under the leadership of their Creator, God.

The devil has done a masterful job of destroying the homes of our times. Today the dysfunctional family is the norm and the normal family that lives Biblical is seen as the dysfunctional unit.

The statistics are everywhere that validate the result of the Romans One Syndrome and its effects on the homes of our times.

What Should We Do?

We must pray and weep over our nation's sin and do like Nehemiah when he heard the news of the condition of Jerusalem, "And it came to pass, when I heard these words, that I sat down and wept, and mourned certain days, and fasted, and prayed before the God of heaven" (Nehemiah 1:4).

The problem too often is we are so busy living life in this Babylonian world we don't care about these matters as we should, therefore we are not serious concerning the great tragedy of our times.

As long as there is life, there is hope, so let us pray and labor in the field of service while we have opportunity to do so. We should labor as if the salvation of others and a nation depended solely upon us doing our duty as the children of God and praying and depending upon God, knowing only He can move in the hearts of people and only He has the power to change hearts that can affect their destiny.

The words that Mordecai sent to Esther are applicable for this time to stand up and speak up for the Lord. "For if thou altogether holdest thy peace at this time, then shall there enlargement and deliverance arise to the Jews from another place; but thou and thy father's house shall be destroyed: and who knoweth whether thou art come to the kingdom for such a time as this" (Esther 4:14).

We can point fingers and blame others, but should we not include ourselves as partly to blame for the Romans One Syndrome and its effect on our world?

Let us join in with Nehemiah as he earnestly prayed over the demise of Jerusalem. "Let thine ear now be attentive, and thine eyes open, that thou mayest hear the prayer of thy servant, which I pray before thee now, day and night, for the children of Israel thy servants, and confess the sins of the children of Israel, which we have sinned against thee: both I and my father's house have sinner" (Nehemiah 1:6).

We must personally break the chains of sins that hold us back from usefulness in the Lord's service. "Wherefore seeing we also are compassed about with so great a cloud of witnesses, let us lay aside every weight, and the sin which doth so easily beset us, and let us run with patience the race that is set before us" (Hebrews 12:1).

We must get serious about the needs of the souls of people around us. We too often fail to see the trees for the forest. By that I mean we let the overall burden of the great need rob us of the sense of urgency to speak to the man or lady next to us of their need of the Saviour.

If there is hope of repentance, it will be one person at a time having their eyes opened to the truth and brought out of the darkness that has blinded them by the power of the new birth.

We should pray for national repentance and a national revival, for as long as there is life there is hope.

We should speak out and speak up, but the chances of our voices being heard above the liberals of our times are slim to none.

Churches are needed that are alive in serving the Lord, that will get back to the fundamentals of the faith and share the gospel with their community and fulfill the complete Great Commission by both, at the same time spreading the gospel around the world through missions and door to door soul winning.

Thank God for the few voices listened to on any level, but the real work that will change a nation is for the individuals that make the homes of that nation to be won to Christ.

Yes, we should speak out to a nation and let our voice be heard to as many as possible declaring the truth of God's Word, but the real change comes about one person at a time experiencing the new birth. "Jesus answered and said unto him, Verily, verily, I say unto thee,

Except a man be born again, he cannot see the kingdom of God" (John 3:3).

Chapter Four

Babylonianism and the Endtimes

To properly and fully understand and appreciate prophecy concerning the endtime and especially the tribulation period, a foundational understanding of Babel and the effect it has had on the world is needed.

The devil has come against God and His plan for humanity from the beginning. Nothing has taken God by surprise for He is omniscient knowing all things. So when we read in the last book of the Bible something recorded that took place before time began for creation, we see He knew the devil's work before it began. Revelation 13:8, "And all that dwell upon the earth shall worship him, whose names are not written in the book of life of the Lamb slain **from the foundation of the world**."

Before sin entered, God had created a utopian world and after all His work, He made man in His image to have fellowship with Him.

The devil, having already rebelled along with a third of heaven's angels, didn't wait long before he came against God by attacking that which was made in His image, man.

We do not know how long after creation's week it was before the devil came to the garden to tempt Eve, but I doubt it was too long. He has always come against God, and the next best thing is man that is made in the image of God.

There in Chapter Three we read of the account of the fall of man as he lost the righteousness with which he had been clothed and set out to make his own covering.

Humanity has yet to cease from attempting to make his own righteous covering but to no avail. Only the blood of the very Son of God can remove our sin and clothe us in His own righteousness.

One of the greatest prophecies is recorded for us at that event in the garden. "And I will put enmity between thee and the woman, and between thy seed and her seed; it shall bruise thy head, and thou shalt bruise his heel" (Genesis 3:15).

For the next 1656 years the devil worked until the flood took them all away. Jesus uses this as an example of when He comes to catch us out of here as seen in Matthew 24:39, "And knew not until the flood came, and took them all away; so shall also the coming of the Son of man be."

It was not long after the flood that the great grandson of Noah from the line of Ham was the next tool used by the devil to come against God's plan.

It appears from the text that in the incident surrounding Noah and his getting drunk that Ham has a character flaw that is seen then in his son Canaan and no doubt the devil found this flaw in his grandson Nimrod, the son of Cush.

May I add this thought here? We do not find a condemnation of Noah but the actions or reactions of Ham and his descendants. After the dissolution of the canopy in the flood, the atmospheric conditions are far different than the world from which Noah had come. I do not think he realized that the grape juice fermented as quickly as it did now in one atmosphere of pressure than when under two.

Also, let us not interject into Scripture what is not written. We do not know what took place, and if we have our idea, we need to preface it with "this is what I think though the Bible doesn't say so." If the Bible is silent, maybe it would be best that we do likewise.

It will be through this man Nimrod that the world will be set on a collision course against God. By whatever means he attains leadership is not clear, but it does say he was a mighty hunter.

Consider this thought. After the ark was emptied of all the animals and their nature was changed due to the change of atmospheric conditions, they would have begun to multiply much more quickly than humanity.

So the wild beast, say a lion or wolf, could have four offspring and that makes six. From them there could be another four next year and from the first generation another four or even eight. Then you would have ten to fourteen, and while a child born would take say 18 to 20 years to manhood, these beasts were now hundreds.

It could well be that the mighty hunter Nimrod provided protection and was seen as a saviour to the people, much as the final Antichrist will be seen by the tribulation peoples.

The white horse rider of the seal judgments is given his crown or position of authority, and Daniel seems to indicate that by craft and the sharing of the booty he will come in peacefully. "And through his policy also he shall cause craft to prosper in his hand; and he shall magnify [himself] in his heart, and by peace shall destroy many: he shall also stand up against the prince of princes; but he shall be broken without hand" (Daniel 8:25).

We are led to believe the earth will be divided into its topographical shape sometime during the life of Peleg.

"And unto Eber were born two sons: the name of one was Peleg; for in his days was the earth divided; and his brother's name was Joktan" (Genesis 10:25).

Some believe this applies only to the division of languages and have ample reasons for that belief. I would not divide fellowship over our differences of views on this matter.

The assumption that a dividing of physical earth would cause a second catastrophic world event is not completely valid as an argument. For instance, what about the time of Joshua's long day?

"And the sun stood still, and the moon stayed, until the people had avenged themselves upon their enemies. Is not this written in the book of Jasher? So the sun stood still in the midst of heaven, and hasted not to go down about a whole day" (Joshua 10:13).

Since we are revolving around the sun, this must mean the crust of the earth ceased to rotate so that from the earth's surface the sun appeared to stand still. This would have caused a great cataclysmic event.

We know that the geological layering of the present world is a result of Noah's flood and the assuaging of the waters. Therefore, the mountains and valleys were separate from that event.

The strata of a geological layer can be found on the next mountain with the matching layer in the valley floor. Most layers can be traced around the entire globe.

So the final division of the physical earth could have occurred many years after the flood as the waters continued to recede.

Peleg was born 99 years after the flood, the fifth from Noah, and Nimrod was fourth from Noah, so we see the time frame for them is similar. Peleg lived 239 years so he died 338 years after the flood. It must have been during that time the earth had its final division.

Abraham was born 185 years after the flood or in the 86th year of Peleg's life, all during the time or just after Nimrod and the building of Babel. Nimrod's kingdom of Babel included the four cities mentioned in Genesis 10:10, "And the beginning of his kingdom was Babel, and Erech, and Accad, and Calneh, in the land of Shinar."

We do not know how long Nimrod lived, but if his life span was similar to those we know, he could well have been alive in the early days of Abraham's life.

Scripture is not clear as to whether Nimrod was the leader of the initial rebellion against God's plan and will, but it is certain that he became the leader at some point.

The rebellion was a consensus of the people, but to accomplish such a task as the tower building required leadership and the organization it provided.

It is during this time the Babylonian Mystery religion was developed and the first stages of humanism began. This makes for a great study, but this I leave for another work in the future.

It was at this time, sometime before the death of Peleg, that the confusion of languages forced people to disperse over the earth, I believe, before it was physically divided. This helps you to understand how all over the globe you find the similarities of histories of people groups and similarities in idol worship or architectural designs such as pyramids and towers dedicated to idol worship.

What I am trying to get across is that the entire world is infected from its roots in Babel, whether it is in religion, its political nature, the idea of globalism, and so on.

The evolutionary mind assumes that some ancient aliens came to this planet and imparted some special knowledge, but I would submit that the only alien would have been fallen angels, and they could have given Nimrod and his contemporaries knowledge, but that would not have been even needed.

Remember the sons of Noah were born in the other world before the flood where the great knowledge was so available. To get an understanding of how knowledge from the Antediluvian world could have been available, Shem lived into the 10th generation that followed him outliving seven of his posterity, even into the 150th year of Abraham's life and the first 50 years of Isaac's.

The Tower of Babel

The purpose of Nimrod's tower was a symbol of defiance against God and His plan to spread out and cover the earth. It was a symbol of rebellion against God's plan. "And the LORD said, Behold, the people is one, and they have all one language; and this they begin to do: and now nothing will be restrained from them, which they have imagined to do" (Genesis 11:6).

A unified effort to rebel by the people against God's plan and the rise of leadership by Nimrod is so much like the majority of today's population and those in leadership of nations.

The knowledge they had and the mindset of rebellion was quickly returning to that of the Antediluvian world, and God stepped in and scattered them abroad by confusing their language.

The devil's goal was to have a one-world system of government and religion. The idolatrous worship was of man's own making, but behind it was the devil at work. Humanism is founded in Babel, the idea that man is his own god in charge of his own future and doesn't have to answer to a Creator God.

Globalism in Babel

They purposed to have internationalism or a global world. Is it not striking that the peoples of the world, whom the greater majority are lost souls, are clamoring for a return to globalism?

The devil's first attempt to unify the world in defiance against God was a global effort, and his last move will be with the same united world at his bidding.

It should not be a surprise that the mysterious movements of a selected few in the world, many of which are rooted centuries deep in history, have the same objective as did this first rebellion against God.

I doubt there to be any mystery as to the goals they aspire to achieve and the numbers they have selected for endtime divisions of the world to match those foretold by the Lord in the Bible.

What man thinks he has devised and is working to achieve is in truth God's design from the start.

"Declaring the end from the beginning, and from ancient times the things that are not yet done, saying, My counsel shall stand, and I will do all my pleasure" (Isaiah 46:10).

Daniel in his prophecy concerning the endtimes and the days of the Antichrist speaks of the fact that the global setting will include ten kingdoms or heads of divisions as seen also in Revelation 17:12.

These are the ten horns seen in the final stages of the image from Daniel's vision in Daniel 7:24.

It will be in that day that the tribulation will come and this last phase of Gentile rule will be destroyed, and the kingdom of God on earth, the millennial reign, will come. "And in the days of these kings shall the God of heaven set up a kingdom, which shall never be destroyed: and the kingdom shall not be left to other people, but it shall break in pieces and consume all these kingdoms, and it shall stand for ever" (Daniel 2:44).

As we watch the world's activities on every level, we cannot help but see the formulating of these infant steps that will grow into the fulfillment of Scripture. We stand at the edge of the dawn of the Day of the Lord.

Chapter 5

Daniel's Three Endtime Gods

Daniel 11:37-39, "Neither shall he regard the God of his fathers, nor the desire of women, nor regard any god: for he shall magnify himself above all. But in his estate shall he honour the God of forces: and a god whom his fathers knew not shall he honour with gold, and silver, and with precious stones, and pleasant things. Thus shall he do in the most strong holds with a strange god, whom he shall acknowledge and increase with glory: and he shall cause them to rule over many, and shall divide the land for gain."

Daniel refers to three endtime gods that will hold sway over the mindset of the world in the days of the Antichrist. These were not the influences that governed the thinking of people in his day but would be the forces controlling the living of people in the times of the Antichrist.

The influence of the old gods will fade away, and there will be new ones that influence the world in the endtime.

I used to think that the phrase "nor the desire of women" meant that the Antichrist would not desire a woman, and that may be true, but notice the context and you will see that he is referring to a god that had an influence on the desire of women, not his desire.

It is true that the world is running rampant towards the acceptance of the homosexual movement to the detriment of society and the impending judgment of God.

To understand what Daniel is saying, we must step out of our modern day world and go back in time to see what the desire of a woman was. What was it that Abraham's wife, Sarah, wanted or desired the most?

Every nation had different names for their fertility gods, but they were under the influence of some god in that day. The insight for us is that in the endtimes there will no longer be this influence.

We are more interested in abortions and preventing fertility than the opposite. So it is evident that this god of Daniel's day is no longer of importance. Once upon a time it was seen as a blessing! It is obvious that the old time god of the desire of women has been replaced for various reasons in our world today.

We no longer need the gods that people looked to for good crops or an abundance of fruit, for we have science and manipulations of genetics to do it for us.

With fertilizers and soil enhancements, we have increased the output of products to an unheard of amount to our grandfathers. It is obvious that the gods of Daniel's day have long ago lost their powers over humanity as a whole.

The God of Forces

Forces that have developed into major controlling influences in our present world are science and technology. Almost every facet of life is influenced by these two forces.

For many, the answer for life's problems that once was sought from a false god is now met with science. We have advanced the average life span by many years. We have a drug for every disease and its symptoms.

It is not difficult to see the power over our daily lives that this god now has over the world. The list would be endless of all the avenues this god has in our world today.

The modern conveniences that technology has given mankind is mighty in its power over our life: from the tractors you farm with that have replaced the single plow and horse, from the invention of radio, telephones, modern television and the computer, and from getting a letter by pony express or ship we can look and talk to each other anywhere in the world at any time.

The nations with early warning systems and advanced armaments are seen as well fortified for both defense and offence. This is due to leading technology.

Through modern day science and technology we are sending pictures back from planet Mars, we walk on the moon and build space stations with our advanced technology, and they say we have proven that there is no God.

The technology of the computer age has an unbelievable power over humanity. So many areas could be examined here that would fill another book.

No doubt this god of forces will be a part of the Antichrist rule over humanity from biotechnology to genetic manipulations of food sources. The list is almost endless of the power this god holds over humanity.

The Unknown God

As Daniel puts it--a god whom his fathers knew not, meaning unknown to his days. This has to be something that has emerged and become a major influence in the entire world that during Daniel's day did not exist, or at least nothing as it will be in the endtimes.

It must be something that did not exist 2,500 years ago but would be a major force of influence over the entire world in the endtimes.

I believe this could be money and a financial system for the entire world. This would have been unknown in Daniel's time.

Notice this god is honored in a different way than the other gods, "shall he honour **with gold, and silver, and with precious stones, and pleasant things.**" The other gods are not rewarded as this god is.

These are things that we place a monetary value on and give to the control of financial markets and in the endtimes will be brought under the power and authority of one person, the Antichrist.

If this were simply an idol, there would be multitudes applying for priestly jobs with these kinds of gifts. So we know it must be more than merely idol worship, though worship and a multitude of followers it has.

If it were a physical god, it would not have the ability to do what this god does for its followers, so it is figurative and unassociated with organized religion from Daniel's day or ours for that fact.

I believe this god is the magical god of money and finance.

The rise of idolatry with money is relatively new to this world. Daniel could see this in his vision but could not recognize it, for it did not exist in his day.

The entire world is reeling over the present collapse of the money and financial woes. They are feverishly trying to find a way to return to the favors this god has given its worshippers for the past few decades.

Many students of prophecy seem to think this will be overseen by the false prophet or the second beast of Revelation. It could well be that a religious economic guru may be the main worship leader for this god, for it will be this person that institutes the mark of the beast and not the first beast or the Antichrist.

Is it not the new gospel of the emergent church movement that is a social gospel coupled with the overwhelming acceptance of the new Christianity for the health and wealth gospel?

I believe there will be a new system of currency and there will be prosperity during the early part of the tribulation.

We see a world today clamoring to achieve a monetary system that is fail proof.

Religion will be a major influence in its final form.

The Babylonian influence of humanism, or the worship of man as his own god, can easily be seen at work on a global scale today. Who better to reward than the god of self and what better reward of our time than a monetary one!

Daniel speaks of the Antichrist having a way of spreading the wealth with the world or sharing the booty, and by craft bringing prosperity to the world.

This may be short lived but rest assured it is coming, but it may not be fully realized until after the rapture when the Antichrist will no longer be restrained by the Holy Spirit living in every believer.

The Strange God

The strange or foreign god is the last one he mentions. By the influence of this god, the Antichrist in the final scenario will be able to break down and bring into subjection even the most defiant of nations. "Thus shall he do in the most strong holds with a strange god."

I believe that by using the influence of the first two gods this god will have an unstoppable power that will end up under the control of this one leader, the Antichrist. "...and he shall cause them to rule over many."

The word strange or foreign means a force from without, from a strange or foreign place, a non-domestic force.

It will be a force that is the greatest of all but interdependent on the others to accomplish and operate. This god will allow the single leader to control the whole population of the earth.

I believe this god to be globalism.

There is not a day that passes that this term is not heard across the world.

The stage is being set for the one-world government, and the use of science and technology, coupled with the money and finance system, will bring the global world into existence for the final Gentile ruler to unite the world against God just as Nimrod did in his day.

A Return to Shinar

In Zechariah's visions, he reveals that just prior to the kingdom of God coming in the millennial something will return to its original roots in Shinar.

Zechariah 5:5-11. "Then the angel that talked with me went forth, and said unto me, Lift up now thine eyes, and see what is this that goeth forth. And I said, What is it? And he said, This is an ephah that goeth forth. He said moreover, This is their resemblance through all the earth. And, behold, there was lifted up a talent of lead: and this is a woman that sitteth in the midst of the ephah. And he said, This is wickedness. And he cast it into the midst of the ephah; and he cast the weight of lead upon the mouth thereof. Then lifted I up mine eyes, and looked, and, behold, there came out two women, and the wind was in their wings; for they had wings like the wings of a stork: and they lifted up the ephah between the earth and the heaven. Then said I to the angel that talked with me, Whither do these bear the ephah? And he said unto me, To build it an house in the land of Shinar: and it shall be established, and set there upon her own base."

This is the seventh of the eight visions he had, and in it we see that prior to the kingdom of God sin returns to Babylon or Shinar.

It was at Shinar that first the sin of rebellion and open disregard for God and His Word is found in the new world after the flood. Genesis 11:1-4, "And the whole earth was of one language, and of one speech. And it came to pass, as they journeyed from the east, that they found a plain in the land of Shinar; and they dwelt there. And they said one to another, Go to, let us make brick, and burn them throughly. And they had brick for stone, and slime had they for morter. And they said, Go to, let us build us a city and a tower, whose top may reach unto heaven; and let us make us a name, lest we be scattered abroad upon the face of the whole earth."

What this woman symbolizes is important.

Zechariah didn't quite get the picture, so he asked what it meant or who this woman was. "And he said, This is wickedness." The scene is this: evil will be carried back to its roots, there to be under submission to the ruling of the Messiah until its final judgment.

The mention of re-establishment is seen in the final statements in Verse 11, "and it shall be established, and set there upon her own base." This seems to be a correlation to the Ziggurat or tower of Babel.

Whether this means a physical rebuilding of Babylon or symbolic of the fact that wickedness is rooted in Babel or Shinar is a debatable matter, but what is clear is that the endtimes are directly tied to the foundations of rebellion at Shinar and Babel.

This is seen in the final judgment of Revelation 16 with the seventh bowl or vial of wrath. Revelation 16:17-19, "And the seventh angel poured out his vial into the air; and there came a great voice out of the temple of heaven, from the throne, saying, It is done. And there were voices, and thunders, and lightnings; and there was a great earthquake, such as was not since men were upon the earth, so mighty an earthquake, and so great. And the great city was divided into three parts, and the cities of the nations fell: and great Babylon came in remembrance before God, to give unto her the cup of the wine of the fierceness of his wrath."

What started in Shinar with Nimrod and Babel has plagued humanity ever since and God has allowed it to remain in force, but in His final plague, He will settle the record and Babylon will be brought into remembrance and destroyed, preparing the way for the millennial reign of Christ.

Chapter 6

The Battle of Psalms 83

Psalms 83:1-18, "Keep not thou silence, O God: hold not thy peace, and be not still, O God For, lo, thine enemies make a tumult: and they that hate thee have lifted up the head. They have taken crafty counsel against thy people, and consulted against thy hidden ones. They have said, Come, and let us cut them off from being a nation; that the name of Israel may be no more in remembrance. For they have consulted together with one consent: they are confederate against thee: The tabernacles of Edom, and the Ishmaelites; of Moab, and the Hagarenes; Gebal, and Ammon, and Amalek; the Philistines with the inhabitants of Tyre; Assur also is joined with them: they have holpen the children of Lot. Selah. Do unto them as unto the Midianites; as to Sisera, as to Jabin, at the brook of Kison: Which perished at Endor: they became as dung for the earth. Make their nobles like Oreb, and like Zeeb: yea, all their princes as Zebah, and as Zalmunna: Who said, Let us take to ourselves the houses of God in possession. O my God, make them like a wheel; as the stubble before the wind. As the fire burneth a wood, and as the flame setteth the mountains on fire; So persecute them with thy tempest, and make them afraid with thy storm. Fill their faces with shame; that they may seek thy name, O LORD. Let them be confounded and troubled for ever; yea, let them be put to shame, and perish:

That men may know that thou, whose name alone is JEHOVAH, art the most high over all the earth."

The signs of this battle are certainly evident today.

The conflict between the Arab peoples and Israel goes all the way back to Abraham and his getting ahead of God and having a son, Ishmael, by the Egyptian handmaid.

Not a day passes but what there is some kind of headline news about the Middle East problem concerning the nations mentioned in this Psalm.

In these verses, a battle is depicted that has never yet taken place. What I have learned in the many years of service to our Lord and the reading and studying of God's Word is that if God has said it then it will come to pass.

Some think this to be a part of the Gog-Magog War, but I believe it is distinctly different. There are several differences between the lists of nations making up the enemy of Israel in these two passages.

Verse 4 tells us that the Arabs want to destroy the *Chosen People*. Is not this the cry of Israel's neighbors today? Psalms 83:12 informs us they want to possess the *Promised Land*.

Thus, Asaph petitioned God for the destruction of this forthcoming enemy league by empowering the Israelites militarily through similar historical examples given in Psalms 83:9-11.

The point surmised is that these enemies want to destroy Israel militarily, so therefore, they should be cursed militarily in like fashion.

There is no evidence that such a regional war uniting ten enemies to the north, east, south, and southeast of Israel ever occurred in ancient times! These were never confederated against Israel in history. This is a future event, and it appears that it is about to play out soon.

Another difficulty of putting this into the Ezekiel 38 battle is that this is namely an *"inner ring"* of Arab nations sharing common borders with Israel, who have been Israel's most observable enemies since 1948, and they are not listed among the Ezekiel invaders.

It could be that the inner ring of Arab states has been defeated by the Israeli Defense Forces prior to the Ezekiel invasion, and therefore the names do not appear on Ezekiel's list.

Nowhere included in Ezekiel's list of populations are Tyre (Lebanon), Asshur (Assyria), Philistia (Gaza), etc. Those populations appear to be reserved for the Psalms 83 Arab – Israeli war.

Dedan is located within the Ezekiel 25:13-15 sequence, which appears to be part of God's response to Psalms 83 and are not a part of the Ezekiel 38 group.

Many recent events lead me to believe, along with many others, that this war is about to take place. We are watching current events that are setting the stage for what has been prophesied for nearly 3,000 years.

If the early part of the tribulation will be where Israel lives in relative peace, then this turmoil and war of Psalms 83 must take place in order to remove the threat of the Arabs against Israel as it now stands.

Anti-Semitism is at an all-time high. When you couple this with the liberal politicians leading the world's governments, the depths of all culture's morals, the forming of political alliances, the economic distress of the entire world, the rise of Islam and all sorts of false religions, and the weakness of true Christianity, you have a world gone mad. Zechariah 12:4, "In that day, saith the LORD, I will smite every horse with astonishment, and his rider with madness: and I will open mine eyes upon the house of Judah, and will smite every horse of the people with blindness."

Many believe in a replacement theology where they teach that the church has replaced Israel and the promises for Israel now belong to the church.

Christians and Church Age saints are to be looking for a heavenly reward that is reserved in glory and that won't fade away (I Peter 1:4). Israel is looking for an earthly reward, the millennial kingdom.

This leads to all sorts of misunderstanding and false teaching concerning the endtimes--dominion theology, post-millennialism, and even a-millennialism, and a dozen other non-scriptural ideas.

The Bible teaches that this world will be ruled by Jesus during the millennium and the church will be in glorified form serving Him, so dominion theology holds no water when compared to Scripture.

The current day names and groups of people may be different than those we find listed, but when you look at the geographical positions, you can see the peoples of today are the ones in Psalms 83. The Palestinians, Hezbollah, and Hamas appear to be enlisted among the ten-member coalition.

Verses 6-8, "The tabernacles of Edom, and the Ishmaelites; of Moab, and the Hagarenes; Gebal, and Ammon, and Amalek; the Philistines with the inhabitants of Tyre; Assur also is joined with them: they have holpen the children of Lot."

Psalms 83 discusses the formation of a ten member, predominately Arab, confederacy destined to someday seek the utter destruction of the nation Israel.

The oil-rich Arab nations have used their energy trump card to get their way against Israel with the Council on Foreign Relations (CFR), the United Nations (U.N.), the European Union (E.U.) and even the United States—all of whom are dependent upon and lust after their oil.

Modern Day Names

These groups named in Psalms 83 were all located surrounding Israel, often seen as to the east. Many were tribes whose moving boundaries often overlapped.

The Tabernacles of Edom

The Tents of Edom refers to the Palestinians of the west bank and southern Jordan.

Jeremiah 49:19, "Behold, he shall come up like a lion **[confederacy of Esau]** from the swelling of Jordan against the habitation of the strong **[Israel]**: but I will suddenly make him run away from her: and who is a chosen man, that I may appoint over her? for who is like me? and who will appoint me the time? and who is that shepherd that will stand before me?"

Obadiah 1:18, "And the house of Jacob shall be a fire, and the house of Joseph a flame, and the house of Esau for stubble, and they shall kindle in them, and devour them; and there shall not be any remaining of the house of Esau; for the LORD hath spoken it."

Israel, represented by the house of Jacob and Joseph, reduces southern Jordan, which is represented by Esau, to rubble. There will be no survivors left as described by Obadiah 1:9. There we see the severity of the judgment in Israel's complete victory over the Palestinian descendants of Edom.

Obadiah 1:9, "And thy mighty men, O Teman, shall be dismayed, to the end that every one of the mount of Esau may be cut off by slaughter."

Teman's modern day equivalent may be Taiwan, about 3 miles east of Petra. Most probably Teman and the mountains of Esau are representative of the entire region of Edom in this passage.

Ezekiel 25:13-14, "Therefore thus saith the Lord GOD; I will also stretch out mine hand upon Edom, and will cut off man and beast from it; and I will make it desolate from Teman; and they of Dedan [**Saudi Arabia**] shall fall by the sword. And I will lay my vengeance upon Edom by the hand of my people Israel: and they shall do in Edom according to mine anger and according to my fury; and they shall know my vengeance, saith the Lord GOD."

This shows the connection to the confederacy from north to south as Esau/Edom [Genesis 36:1] are interchangeable words for the same peoples, as is Ishmaelites with Ishmael and Israelites are to Jacob [Genesis 32:28].

The army of Israel will advance beyond the southern border of Jordan into northwest Saudi Arabia as far south as the Red Sea.

Ishmael

Ishmael was the eponymous father of the Arabs, his brother Isaac being the father of the Jews. The Ishmaelites most probably refer to the Saudi Arabians, but that identification is admittedly speculative for it may refer to Arabs in general.

Jeremiah 49:8, "Flee ye, turn back, dwell deep, O inhabitants of Dedan [**Saudi Arabia**]; for I will bring the calamity of Esau upon him, the time that I will visit him [**southern Jordan**]."

Moab

These are the present day Palestinian Refugees and Central Jordanians. Jeremiah 48:46-47, "Woe be unto thee, O Moab! the people of Chemosh perisheth: for thy sons are taken captives, and thy daughters captives. Yet will I bring again the captivity of Moab in the latter days, saith the LORD. Thus far is the judgment of Moab."

The Hagarites

The Hagarites correspond with the land of Egypt.

Isaiah 19:18-19, "In that day shall five cities in the land of Egypt speak the language of Canaan, and swear to the LORD of hosts; one shall be called, The city of destruction. In that day shall there be an altar to the LORD in the midst of the land of Egypt, and a pillar at the border thereof to the LORD."

Isaiah tells us that the expansion of Israeli control in the region will even reach into Egypt to some degree. Five Hebrew-speaking cities will be established in the land of Egypt. There will be an altar erected to God as well as a pillar erected to God on the border.

One of the last pieces to fall in place is the Islamic Brotherhood's takeover of Egypt. The military takeover and the exclusion of the brotherhood may lead to further civil war. It is putting the Muslim Brotherhood in bed with the terrorist of Gaza.

And this may help lead to the re-establishment of the caliphate centered in Turkey for the king of the South in Daniel's prophecy of the final four Kings at the end of Gentile rule.

Could the prophesy of Egypt found in Ezekiel 29:8-12 be fulfilled in this coming war with the use of a nuclear device?

"Therefore thus saith the Lord GOD; Behold, I will bring a sword upon thee, and cut off man and beast out of thee. And the land of Egypt shall be desolate and waste; and they shall know that I am the LORD: because he hath said, The river is mine, and I have made it. Behold, therefore I am against thee, and against thy rivers, and I will make the land of Egypt utterly waste and desolate, from the tower of Syene even unto the border of Ethiopia. No foot of man shall pass through it, nor foot of beast shall pass through it, neither shall it be inhabited forty years. And I will make the land of Egypt desolate in the midst of the countries that are desolate, and her cities among the cities that are laid waste shall be desolate forty years: and I will scatter the Egyptians among the nations, and will disperse them through the countries."

At the head of the Nile River, the tower of Syene is where the Aswan Dam sits. The greatest majority of the food grown in Egypt comes from the Nile River basin.

If in this war Israel dropped an atomic bomb on the dam, the river would become fertile and the crop land would lay waste 400 miles down into Ethiopia. Ethiopia is threatening to dam up the Nile now, which may also play into the final scenario.

That would render Egypt impotent and dependent upon outside help or perish. Though they know this, the blindness of the Islamic religion would cause them to risk all to wipe Israel off the map, and if they do, I doubt that Israel will allow the world's pressure to prevent them from doing just that.

"As the fire burneth a wood, and as the flame setteth the mountains on fire, so persecute them with Thy tempest and make them afraid with Thy storm."

Egypt will probably meet her demise as a threat as a result of this war and not be a part of the Ezekiel 38-39 War.

Gebal

This corresponds with Hezbollah and the Lebanese as they border Israel today.

They are working feverishly now at arming themselves with the aid of Iran, funneling arms through Syria.

Even supplies from Russia are being smuggled into these people, and it is said they have 10,000 rockets pointed at Israel now.

Ammon

This includes the Palestinians and northern Jordanians. Jordan became a nation in 1946, but prior to this was referred to down through the generations as Edom, Moab, and Ammon.

Jeremiah 49:2, "Therefore, behold, the days come, saith the LORD, that I will cause an alarm of war to be heard in Rabbah of the Ammonites [**Ammon, Jordan**]; and it shall be a desolate heap, and her daughters shall be burned with fire: then shall Israel be heir unto them that were his heirs, saith the LORD."

Much of modern-day Jordan was once part of the inheritance of Israel. The tribes of east Manasseh, Benjamin, Gad, and Reuben once possessed land that is presently under Jordanian control. There is a time coming when this land will come back to its rightful owner.

Jeremiah 49:3-6, "Howl, O Heshbon, for Ai is spoiled: cry, ye daughters of Rabbah, gird you with sackcloth; lament, and run to and fro by the hedges; for their king shall go into captivity, and his priests and his princes together. Wherefore gloriest thou in the valleys, thy flowing valley, O backsliding daughter? that trusted in her treasures, saying, Who shall come unto me? Behold, I will bring a fear upon thee, saith the Lord GOD of hosts, from all those that be about thee; and ye shall be driven out every man right forth; and none shall gather up him that wandereth. And afterward I will bring again the captivity of the children of Ammon, saith the LORD."

Amalek

These are the Arabs that live south of Israel, some inside their own borders and those in part of Saudi Arabia.

Phillistia

This corresponds with Hamas and the Gaza Strip of our day, the ancient land of the Philistines that Israel had so much trouble with through the Old Testament records.

Obadiah 1:19, "And they of the south shall possess the mount of Esau **[southern Jordan]**; and they of the plain the Philistines **[Gaza Strip]**: and they shall possess the fields of Ephraim, and the fields of Samaria **[west bank]**: and Benjamin shall possess Gilead **[west bank and Golan Heights]**."

The attempt at a peace treaty is a futile effort and may set the stage upon failure to engage in this war.

The Inhabitants of Tyre

This corresponds to Hezbollah and southern Lebanon. There is much distress in this area as Syria's civil war is spreading towards Israel.

This conflict may well trigger this war described for us in Psalms 83 as Israel preemptively strikes the weapons transfer to these terrorists.

The Golan Heights will be a point of contention for peace talks because Israel cannot afford to give up this buffer zone of protection.

Assur - Assyria

Last but not least is Assyria (Syria and Kurdish Iraq).

Though Persia or modern day Iran is not mentioned, they are part of the force behind this effort to annihilate Israel through their surrogates of Hamas and Hezbollah, located in Jordan, Lebanon, Syria, Gaza, and the west bank.

Iran or Persia is not Arab. They are distant cousins of the Europeans. They share the same religion of Islam, but they are the Shiite believers, whereas the majority of the Arabs based in Mecca in Saudi Arabia are Sunnis.

Through their surrogates of Hamas, Palestinians, Hezbollah, Brotherhood of Arabs and so many smaller Jihadist groups, they now have a complete circle of power around Israel just as described for us in this Psalm.

The present Syrian conflict is spilling over into the regions, and Israel is being forced to do preemptive strikes. With this may come the tool used by the other nation in this prophecy to unite and come against Israel.

Left to itself, Syria may well be dissolved from the civil war and be broken up into the border nation without Israel's involvement. Only time will tell.

Syria, or Damascus its capital and often used symbolically for the nation, is not mentioned in the Ezekiel 38 battle, maybe because after the Psalms 83 battle or its present inner turmoil by that time will be irrelevant.

Turkey and the Caliphate

We are seeing the reforming of the Islamic Caliphate with the old Ottoman Empire. It has never really been a friend to the west because it is Islamic to its core. With their present leadership, they are returning to the Islamic rule and will no doubt set up a ruling headquarters again.

The Arab Spring, as it has been referred to, is setting the course for these nations under extreme Islamic control to come under this controlling and unifying rule.

They have used the west to rebuild their infrastructure, financial institution, their military, and wealth, and now they will break away and return to their old religious motives of dominating the world. They hate Israel as much as any other nation in the Middle East.

They know that even with their great military they would have a difficult time defeating Israel and doubt they could, so they play the game of fence straddling trying to satisfy their Islamic brothers and have a so-called peace with Israel.

Time will come when they will join the others in an all-out war on Israel. This will probably not be with this war but the one that follows.

When this battle is over, Israel will be elevated to a condition of regional superiority due to their decisive victory over the Arab confederacy. As such, they dwell securely in the Middle East. This could be the scene that precedes the battle of Ezekiel 38-39 as the Antichrist will be rising up at this time.

A Final Thought

The stage is well set for this conflict. All fronts are ready to come against Israel. We have become so concerned about Iran that we have built missile defense systems to protect these Arab nations, and now we see they may well be used as defense against Israel, but to no avail.

So here we have all of Israel's next door neighbors, all of them sworn to Israel's destruction, and all of them being whipped into a frenzy by Syria and Iran through her surrogates. And now Egypt and even Turkey are pondering their role in all this.

It seems that this battle is an inner ring of Arab Islamic countries where as Ezekiel 38 is an outer ring of non-Arab Islamic nations.

Given current events, I would not be surprised if before this is printed this battle could take place. When this war takes place, the world will be stunned. The little nation of Israel will have extended its borders many times over and subdued the Arab nations, and Islam will take a great setback.

Jeremiah 49:20-21, "Therefore hear the counsel of the LORD, that he hath taken against Edom; and his purposes, that he hath purposed against the inhabitants of Teman: Surely the least of the flock shall draw them out: surely he shall make their habitations desolate with them. The earth is moved at the noise of their fall, at the cry the noise thereof was heard in the Red sea."

Isaiah puts it like this in Isaiah 17:12-13, "Woe to the multitude of many people, which make a noise like the noise of the seas; and to the rushing of nations, that make a rushing like the rushing of mighty waters! The nations shall rush like the rushing of many waters: but God shall rebuke them, and they shall flee far off, and shall be chased as the chaff of the mountains before the wind, and like a rolling thing before the whirlwind."

A map of the lands of Psalms 83 both then and now. You can see the enlargement that will take place after the war is over.

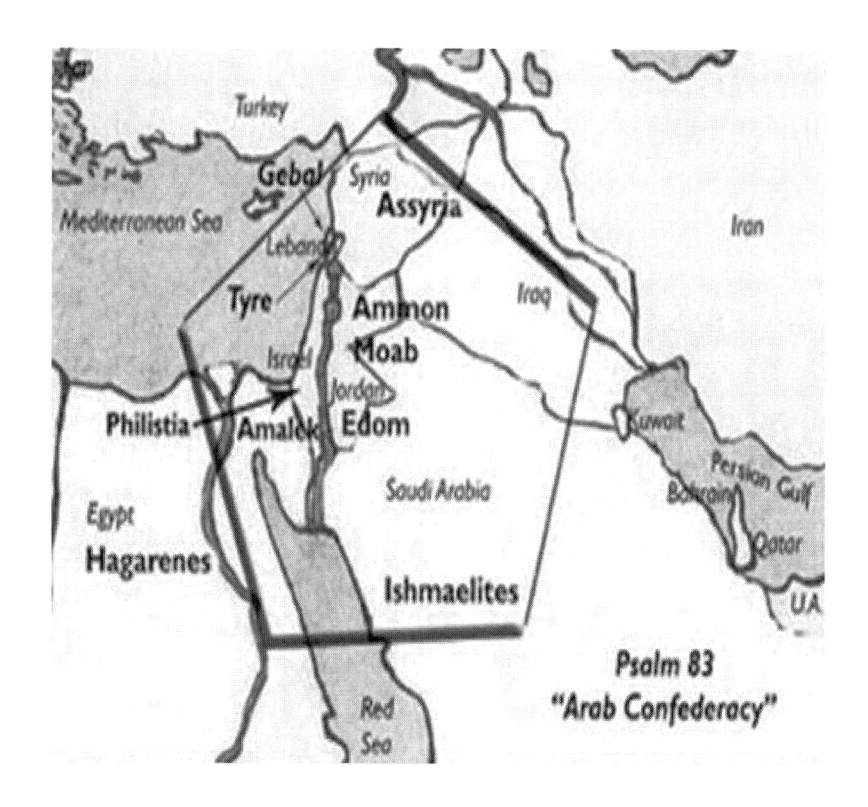

Chapter 7

Ezekiel 38 Allies and Outcome

You do not need to look too hard to see the alignment of these nations forming alliances with each other with Russia forming the lead for them.

Most of our attention is upon Persia, or Iran as it is called today. They are a peculiar people. They are not Arabs but of European descent and hold the religion of the Arabs, Islam.

To a certain degree, there is an underlying hatred of the Persians by the Arab nations for what they perceive as having their religion's prominence stolen from them.

Though the Islamic Muslims will fight with each other against the infidels and the Jews, they also fight amongst themselves as fiercely.

To a certain degree, Israel and the west have been able to use this as leverage to keep as much of the conflict as low as possible.

The tide though is shifting as the uneasiness in the Middle East is rising on every front. Not a day passes without major news of some activity stirring the pot there.

It is like a pot of water on the stove. As it heats, it begins to send out steam and a little bubble here and there, so you stir it and it sort of settles down. But eventually the stirring will bring it to a boiling point that cannot be stopped.

Between each stirring, the period of calm gets shorter, and then it erupts. This is what is happening now. How long before it erupts only the Lord in heaven knows, but it certainly is heating up.

There is much debate concerning the who, when, why, where, and the how of this battle to come. There may be disagreement over some of the elements of this issue, but there is agreement that it is coming and the outcome is certain.

No one author, researcher, preacher, theologian, professor, or anyone else will settle the difference in views, for there are certain areas of Scripture and especially in prophecy that are very subjective, for there are places where Scripture is silent or symbolic.

I, like many, have had a change in view over the past 47 years of ministry as new light has come on the scene, and more understanding of Scripture has secured my thoughts. But I do not think we should be dogmatic and authoritative in areas where silence in Scripture is found.

We need to let the Scripture have authority in our lives and not take authority over Scripture where these matters are not declared clearly by God.

We will attempt to address in a short overview the questions of **who, when, why, where, and the how** of this subject.

I realize there are very learned and studied men with more years of intensive research in this field than I have, and I do not claim to know all truth in such matters.

I simply will state what I personally believe concerning these areas and do not seek to cause division or discord or animosity among the brethren.

The Who

Ezekiel 38:1-6, "And the word of the LORD came unto me, saying, Son of man, set thy face against Gog, the land of Magog, the chief prince of Meshech and Tubal, and prophesy against him, And say, Thus saith the Lord GOD; Behold, I am against thee, O Gog, the chief prince of Meshech and Tubal: And I will turn thee back, and put hooks into thy jaws, and I will bring thee forth, and all thine army, horses and horsemen, all of them clothed with all sorts of armour, even a great company with bucklers and shields, all of them handling swords: Persia, Ethiopia, and Libya with them; all of them with shield and helmet: Gomer, and all his bands; the house of Togarmah of the north quarters, and all his bands: and many people with thee. Son of man, set thy face against Gog, the land of Magog, the chief prince of Meshech and Tubal."

The When

Ezekiel 38:8, "After many days thou shalt be visited: in the latter years thou shalt come into the land that is brought back from the sword, and is gathered out of many people, against the mountains of Israel, which have been always waste: but it is brought forth out of the nations, and they shall dwell safely all of them."

This is a matter of discussion no doubt since the second century. If Bible students and preachers down through the ages were anything like those of us today, and I would think they were, then they discussed this issue without a common consensus also.

There is more than one view concerning the *when* of this battle. No one doubts there is a battle, though some would seem to think it in history, and they think we are living in the millennial time. If that be true, then there seems to be a lot of things going on that, if Christ is on the throne, just does not fit so much of other Scripture.

Among those in the futurist camp there are two main thoughts. One sees it before the tribulation, the other within the tribulation. Then some see it as the Armageddon battle or as a pre-battle up to it.

At least within our circles we agree it is future and a real battle to come.

Both the before and during the tribulation views have credible arguments. As to whether before or after the rapture, only God knows since the rapture has been imminent since 70 AD.

We are seeing the staging of this battle being set up in our times. The countries are certainly aligning themselves for this joint effort. Hardly a day passes without some major news release that applies to this matter.

It could well happen before the tribulation since there are several other factors besides the rapture that must come into play before the Antichrist rides a white horse of peace.

Too often we see the signs of the endtimes and forget they are for the tribulation and not the rapture. Many have the misconception that the rapture of the saints and the ending of the Church Age is the trigger that starts the tribulation, but this is not what is taught in the Bible.

I can easily find ten things in the Scripture that must take place before the tribulation period begins, and there might be a couple others I missed. Four have been fulfilled and six to go.

One of them is the rapture, for I believe the Bible teaches clearly that we will be caught out of here prior to the tribulation.

1. WW I - the trigger starting the beginning of the ending of this age.
2. The re-establishment of Israel.
3. Jerusalem under Jewish control (including the revival of their language).
4. The battle of Psalms 83.
5. The Ezekiel 38-39 battle.
6. The one-world government.
7. The ten kingdoms formed.
8. The rapture (at any moment placed here only because it must precede the next).
9. The rise of the Antichrist (after the rapture – II Thessalonians 2:6-8).
10. A time of peace leading to a peace treaty.

So when will it take place? Only God knows for certain, but we can see there is time remaining before the tribulation begins, and with the events occurring in the Middle East now, it would indicate that it could well be prior to the tribulation.

I know that Daniel speaks of pushing the king of the north and south against the king of the west seen as the Antichrist, and it appears that it is in the tribulation time. But a closer look at Daniel could also indicate this pushing could be partly prior to the tribulation.

Do I think the king of the west is America? The answer in its final days for the tribulation is a definite no. I know many think America will be as much a player in the end days as we have been for the last few decades.

Daniel spoke of the ten toes or kingdoms and John wrote of the ten mountains or kingdoms. For the past few decades, America has been the big toe of the world, so either nine more must come up or we will go down in power and prominence.

Only a blind person or one unwilling to look would not see the latter is what is happening in our present time.

There certainly is a lot of jockeying in the world right now for the position of leadership, both militarily and economically.

I do not think this battle to come is the same as the Psalms 83 battle, which was discussed before in the previous chapter.

That battle could lead to this one, for if Israel is seen as rendering a great defeat to the Arab nations that surrounds them, though we know it will be of God's doing, a brief similitude of peace could be what is referred to as the setting for the Ezekiel 38-39 war.

Or as some point out, the peace treaty starting the tribulation is that which precedes this war.

Given the current stirrings of these nations, it could well happen sooner than later. The ominous signs of these things to come are everywhere you turn today.

All this should motivate us as God's people to dedicate ourselves anew to take the gospel to a lost world for time is growing short.

The Why

Ezekiel 38:10-12, "Thus saith the Lord GOD; It shall also come to pass, that at the same time shall things come into thy mind, and thou shalt think an evil thought And thou shalt say, I will go up to the land of unwalled villages; I will go to them that are at rest, that dwell safely, all of them dwelling without walls, and having neither bars nor gates, To take a spoil, and to take a prey; to turn thine hand upon the desolate places that are now inhabited, and upon the people that are gathered out of the nations, which have gotten cattle and goods, that dwell in the midst of the land."

The answer is simple - to take a spoil. The Lord will cause them to think this evil, so He once again will make a statement to Israel and the world that He is God.

Israel will be in some sort of peace or in a sense of confidence that God will cause these nations to think this is the time to come against Israel. Ezekiel 38:14, "Therefore, son of man, prophesy and say unto Gog, Thus saith the Lord GOD; In that day when my people of Israel dwelleth safely, <u>shalt thou not know it</u>?"

Russia has been the great supplier of natural gas to Europe and the east for a long time, and they want to remain the dominant force both in this and militarily.

With the recent discoveries in Israel of the natural gas field that may be the largest ever and the oil field of great enormity, it seems that Russia may want these to maintain dominance.

This is God's Doings

Ezekiel 38:4, "And I will turn thee back, and put hooks into thy jaws, and I will bring thee forth, and all thine army, horses and horsemen, all of them clothed with all sorts of armour, even a great company with bucklers and shields, all of them handling swords."

What these hooks may be, again it is not so clear, but it is God that by these means causes these invaders to think about coming and taking Israel's spoil. Have you noticed that in the many events of the endtimes, and especially the tribulation after the restraint of the Holy Spirit is removed, that man thinks he is guiding his own affairs when in truth it is simply God's foretold plan that is unfolding?

It will not be difficult to get the nations that are mentioned to come along under the leadership of Russia since they are mostly non-Arab Islamic peoples who feel a sense of duty to fight against Israel after they have defeated the inner ring of Arab fellow Islamic nations.

But it is Russia that no doubt provides the major military knowhow and equipment, and most of these nations have all the energy source they need and will gladly let Russia have the rest.

These Islamic nations, like all of Islam, hate the west and Israel and have vowed to the death to destroy them. They may come close, but in the end, it will be they that are destroyed by God's intervention and not man's.

Is it not amazing that after the many times that God demonstrates His power and defeats the enemies of God's people that they still do not return unto Him?

There are many times in Scripture where God delivers and His mighty hand is evident yet men do not seem to recognize it or acknowledge it.

An example is in Chapter 16 of Revelation where at least twice men are experiencing the divine judgment of God. They know it is of His doing and they still in defiance blaspheme God.

One can easily see how the Lord could cause it to come into the thinking of Russia to come for the great spoil as well as the involvement of these Islamic nations mentioned as mentioned here.

The Where

Ezekiel 38:8, "After many days thou shalt be visited: in the latter years thou shalt come into the land that is brought back from the sword, and is gathered out of many people, against the mountains of Israel, which have been always waste: but it is brought forth out of the nations, and they shall dwell safely all of them."

Ezekiel 39:4, "Thou shalt fall upon the mountains of Israel, thou, and all thy bands, and the people that is with thee: I will give thee unto the ravenous birds of every sort, and to the beasts of the field to be devoured."

Though there is much language in the verses surrounding these two that are certainly compatible to those in the events of tribulation in Revelation, it could cause one to think it to take place within that time's frame.

As some believe it to be the final battle of the tribulation referred to as Armageddon, there are yet other things about it that appear that it is not. It could well be that the two battles are closely connected or the last follow up result of this battle.

Two Different Groups – Two Different Places

The differences are seen in the peoples of the two battles. They are of different nations and the purpose of God for the two are not the same.

Ezekiel 39:1-2. "Therefore, thou son of man, prophesy against Gog, and say, Thus saith the Lord GOD; Behold, I am against thee, O Gog, the chief prince of Meshech and Tubal: And I will turn thee back, and leave but the sixth part of thee, and will cause thee to come up from the north parts, and will bring thee upon the mountains of Israel."

This battle seems to be God dealing with these nations, and especially Russia, for a long standing judgment that has been intended for them from past crimes against God and His people. The last battle will be with many other nations especially the king of the west and the king of the east and at the valley of Jehoshaphat. Its purpose seems to be directly related to another reason other than the one in this battle.

Here it is for a booty, and the final battle is for ultimate control of the world, especially Israel, and it is for God's righteous judgment against those nations that have been guilty of causing Israel to part God's land.

Joel 3:2, "I will also gather all nations, and will bring them down into the valley of Jehoshaphat, and will plead with them there for my people and for my heritage Israel, whom they have scattered among the nations, and parted my land."

The *where* of these two battles seems to be at different locations as well as the peoples or nations. The location of the first seems to be a descending from the north and east where the last battle seems to be the nations that have through these last days caused or had a part in causing Israel to give up the land God promised Abraham in the so-called peace process prior to this time.

The first battle with Russia as the leader leaves them with a sixth of the army left. Ezekiel 39:2, "And I will turn thee back, and leave but the sixth part of thee, and will cause thee to come up from the north parts, and will bring thee upon the mountains of Israel."

The last battle leaves no one left and seems to be associated with the final bowl of wrath, the destruction of Babylon and the reshaping of the world for the Millennial Reign of Christ.

To me, it certainly seems that the two battles are different on several counts.

1. The peoples are different.
2. The places are different.
3. The purpose for the peoples gathered is different.
4. The outcome is different.
5. They will bury the dead after the first battle, not the second.

Other differences could be seen, and I would be remiss if I did not say there are some similarities. The overall conclusion that I have reached is that they are two separate events with two separate peoples for two different purposes of God.

The How

As to how much of the description of this battle is symbolic and what is literal is also a debatable subject.

Many factors could come into play that might render armies incapable of modern weaponry at that time and more of it could be literal than we might think. We live in a computer-controlled world and modern weapons are dependent upon satellites, which could be rendered useless by a super surge of energy in the upper atmosphere by God's using the sun or man using an atomic bomb in the heavens.

This may be another reason to think this battle is associated with the red horse rider of the second seal judgment.

The result of the great number of deaths to the enemy could also be from weapons of mass destruction or simply the power of God.

God has demonstrated many times his power in these matters without the aid of human involvement.

Sennacherib, king of Assyria, found out the power of one angel in II Chronicles 32:21, "And the LORD sent an angel, which cut off all the mighty men of valour, and the leaders and captains in the camp of the king of Assyria. So he returned with shame of face to his own land. And when he was come into the house of his god, they that came forth of his own bowels slew him there with the sword. Thus the LORD saved Hezekiah and the inhabitants of Jerusalem from the hand of Sennacherib the king of Assyria, and from the hand of all other, and guided them on every side."

It is evident that it will be a divine intervention.

Ezekiel 39:2, "And <u>I will</u> turn thee back, and leave but the sixth part of thee, <u>and will</u> cause thee to come up from the north parts, <u>and will</u> bring thee upon the mountains of Israel."

Ezekiel 39:3, "And <u>I will</u> smite thy bow out of thy left hand, and will cause thine arrows to fall out of thy right hand."

Ezekiel 39:6, "And <u>I will</u> send a fire on Magog, and among them that dwell carelessly in the isles: and they shall know that I am the LORD."

Five times it says that God will do this. The reason is clear "and they shall know that I am the LORD."

I am amazed at all the times and things that God has done and will do on behalf of Israel, and yet they still remain in blindness and will until that fateful day when the Lord of glory appears in the eastern sky, coming to end the tribulation and set up His kingdom just like Daniel pictured it all those centuries ago.

Daniel 2:34-35, "Thou sawest till that a stone was cut out without hands, which smote the image upon his feet that were of iron and clay, and brake them to pieces. Then was the iron, the clay, the brass, the silver, and the gold, broken to pieces together, and became like the chaff of the summer threshingfloors; and the wind carried them away, that no place was found for them: and the stone that smote the image became a great mountain, and filled the whole earth."

I tend to lean more towards the literal interpretation of the Bible as a whole rather than the allegorical method used by so many.

The greater majority of Bible commentaries that are so trustworthy and sound written many years ago seem to use both the symbolism method as well as a historical view.

I find it interesting how they try to view so much from a historical position yet often try to hold to a premillennial tribulation and rapture view at the same time.

It does seem that writers from before World War I tend to have more of a historist slant than those after the re-establishment of Israel. I suppose more light on the endtimes does make a difference, yet no one can claim to know all there is to learn from these times.

I tend to be more of a literalist and futurist holding to the premillennial and pretribulational rapture view.

This does not mean that historically there have not been similar events that appear to be fulfillment, but what is often overlooked is that prophecies often have a dual purpose or a first and secondary fulfillment.

This could be applied to some events, but to this battle of Ezekiel 38 and 39 is future.

The Outcome

When this battle is over, God will have once again shown Himself mighty on the behalf of Israel. Yet like so many times in their ancient history and even recent history, they are blind to the truth.

Paul was right when he wrote under the inspiration of the Holy Spirit these words in Romans 11:25, "For I would not, brethren, that ye should be ignorant of this mystery, lest ye should be wise in your own conceits; that blindness in part is happened to Israel, until the fulness of the Gentiles be come in."

Not until the last of the Gentile rulers are defeated will Israel be able to see this truth. Revelation 1:7, "Behold, he cometh with clouds; and every eye shall see him, and they also which pierced him: and all kindreds of the earth shall wail because of him. Even so, Amen."

Zechariah 12:10, "And I will pour upon the house of David, and upon the inhabitants of Jerusalem, the spirit of grace and of supplications: and they shall look upon me whom they have pierced, and they shall mourn for him, as one mourneth for his only son, and shall be in bitterness for him, as one that is in bitterness for his firstborn."

The kings of the north and south will be delivered a great blow and maybe rendered almost irrelevant for the remainder of the tribulation after this battle.

They may be reassembled to take part in the final battle, but it is evident to me that the major players of the final battle are the other two kingdoms of peoples.

Another result of this may be the emboldening of the king of the east to make her run against the west for final dominance of the world, only there to unite to battle God and be destroyed.

This is another reason I personally think it will be in the tribulation time frame, though it could precede it.

Conclusion

We seem to be standing at the edge of the dawning of the Day of the Lord as the signs of the endtimes are abundant.

The signs of the ending days of the Church Age are plentiful and obvious to the spiritual eye. Even the lost world seems to know that there is change in the wind.

They run to all sorts of pagan resources looking for answers but refuse to take the infallible truth of the matter from the Bible.

Many Christians are fearful of these times when they should be excited. This is simply because they do not understand what is really going on.

I pray that this little treatise on the subject will help those that read it.

There are many more signs written about here and multitudes of evidences related to these subjects that are available to those looking for them.

Keep your eyes on the Middle East and especially Israel. Keep your ears tuned for the shout from heaven for at any moment He could say come up hither.

People often ask if I think things will improve and I say if they do, it will be but for a short time and then be worse than before.

We must keep our focus on the right purpose, and it has never changed and that is the Great Commission. Mark 16:15, "And he said unto them, Go ye into all the world, and preach the gospel to every creature."

The hope for our times is still the gospel, and the only ones that can rightfully share that good news are the people that have experienced it.

We need to realize the shortness of time and get serious about serving the Lord and laying up treasures in heaven instead of on this earth.

When the tribulation is over, the rewards you have earned in this life will be made crowns that we may cast at the feet of our Saviour and praise Him for His grace, mercy, and love.

These rewards will be translated into responsibilities in the service of the Lord throughout the Millennial and evidently in the new heavens and earth that is to come. Revelation 20:6, "Blessed and holy is he that hath part in the first resurrection: on such the second death hath no power, but they shall be priests of God and of Christ, and shall reign with him a thousand years." Also see Revelation 22:1-5.

So we should desire to work and labor to receive rewards so we can enjoy our eternal service at its fullest.

We need to take a close look at what the Bible says about that eternity to come. When the Millennial Reign is over and the final judgment of God and the Great White Throne of Judgment is finished, this present universe will be remade for eternity absent of sin.

To enjoy eternity with no reason to shed a tear, God will do one last thing for us before that new world begins.

Revelation 21:4, "And God shall wipe away all tears from their eyes; and there shall be no more death, neither sorrow, nor crying, neither shall there be any more pain: for the former things are passed away."

Simply, He will remove from our remembrance every one that is not in heaven. There would be tears if in a million years one day we thought of someone we now love is perishing in eternal damnation in the lake of fire, so God will wipe their remembrance from our minds.

All those that are not in heaven will forever be forgotten by those that are.

As you close this book, will you bow your head and close your eyes and visualize some person or persons that you love and care for deeply, that you know are not saved, and get that image burned into your mind?

Now ask the Lord to embolden and enable you to reach them with the gospel before it is too late. Get a burden that you would rather not eat or do anything of pleasure more than to see them saved.

Dedicate and consecrate yourself to the business of seeing them know Jesus as Saviour. For the only people that will inhabit eternal bliss in glory are those that have their names written in the Lamb's Book of Life.

About the Author

Dr. Charles Hiltibidal was born in a lay preacher's home in 1948. He grew up in rural southern Illinois and after 47 years of ministry, he has returned to live on the family farm with his wife, Mary, of 45 years.

He started the New Testament Baptist Church of Centralia, Illinois, after many years of assistant pastor and music director positions in three churches. He pastored the Grace Baptist Temple of Duncanville, Texas, and served there almost 18 years. He recently resigned his pastorate of Grace Baptist Church of Raleigh, Illinois, a rural church twenty-four miles from the farm, where he pastored over ten years.

The ministry grew under his leadership from less than a dozen people to an average of 90-100 with a printing ministry, an aggressive weekly outreach including busses and vans and various children's ministries, a strong missions' program, and a sound Bible-centered church family.

He is also on the executive board of directors of the Creation Evidences Museum of Glen Rose, Texas, which started as a result of the ministry of the Grace Baptist Temple where he pastored.

His son, Mark Hiltibidal is now his pastor and the church is moving forward reaching new heights in every area of ministry. He retains the position of pastor emeritus of Grace Baptist Church and is privileged to represent them in his travels.

He is now actively involved as an evangelist helping local churches especially in the areas of both science & Bible and prophecy. His many years in the ministry with its varied involvement in Archeology and Bible study as well as practical ministry in the local church has given him an insight into the Word of God in a unique way.

By applying archeological discoveries, scientific evidences for creation, historical documentation, prophecy fulfilled and yet to come with the Scriptures brings the Bible to life as he takes a church from eternity past through time to eternity future.

His ministry through Grace Baptist is called "Walk Through Time Ministries."

Reference Materials for This Book

God's Word, the King James Bible

Adam Clarke's Commentary

Albert Barnes' NT Commentary

William Burkitt's Notes on the New Testament

Robertson's NT Word Pictures

Various research and study of over forty years

Various articles and writings from the internet

News outlets

Web sites:

Rapture Ready News
Prophecy news Watch
Prophecy in the News
Prophecy Truth
Lamb & Lion Ministries
Eternal Value Review
And a few others of lesser importance to this study.

Other materials are available through the web site www.wttministries.com.

Books written by this author can be ordered directly through the website as well as audio teaching on both science and the Bible and prophecy.

You may contact us through the web site or by email charleshiltibidal@yahoo.com.

Mailing address:
Dr. Charles Hiltibidal
R. R. 2, Box 463
McLeansboro, IL 62859